GHOSTS
of Gettysburg

IX

Spirits, Apparitions and Haunted Places of the Battlefield

by
Mark Nesbitt

Second Chance Publications
Gettysburg, PA 17325

To Carol,
Again and Forever....

'She'll stay.
She will never go away again.
The Lost Princess is lost no more.
This is her home now—of
Her own free will.'"

—Paul Gallico, *The Snow Goose*

TABLE OF CONTENTS

The Lost Files 1

A Familiar Voice from Beyond 3

A Haunted Highway 7

South of Gettysburg...13

Walking Shadows..27

The Ghost House...Again..35

Spangler's Meadow 55

Horrors Beyond Horrors..69

Where Dreams Came to Die...87

Hell Night 103

Harvesting Souls in the Wheatfield.............................121

The Noisy Ghosts of Gettysburg...................................139

Acknowledgments...155

About the Author...157

"The only thing we learn from history is that we won't learn from history."

—Georg Hegel

"You cannot learn anything from history if they keep erasing inconvenient history."

—Carol Nesbitt

THE LOST FILES

I began collecting ghost stories of Gettysburg as a Park Ranger in 1970. I published the first *Ghosts of Gettysburg* book in 1991. When this first book came out, I believed it would be the *only* book on ghosts and the supernatural tales of Gettysburg that I would write.

I was shocked when, within two weeks of its initial release, I began getting letters, phone calls, faxes (yes, it was *that* long ago!) from people writing to tell me the story of their ghostly encounters at Gettysburg. Stories continued to pour in. Seven more volumes followed the first.

Since the first volume I moved twice and bought the house on the corner of Baltimore and Breckenridge Streets in Gettysburg from which we operate the "Ghosts of Gettysburg Candlelight Walking Tours." File cabinets and boxes of folders began to spread out between the buildings.

This is how the stories in those folders became "lost."

I wasn't sure I would write a *Ghosts of Gettysburg IX*. Then I re-discovered the file folders filled with eyewitness reports of paranormal encounters at Gettysburg.

You can imagine the pleasure with which I perused this "new" batch of first-person, eyewitness accounts of supernatural events from years past. They form the core of *Ghosts of Gettysburg IX*.

A FAMILIAR VOICE FROM BEYOND

When that this body did contain a spirit,
A kingdom for it was too small a bound...

—Shakespeare, *Henry IV*

Ghost research is, fundamentally, the attempt to find proof of life after death.

All research, study, collecting of evidence and analysis strives—or should strive—towards one fundamental goal: To prove that when we die, we—our "selves"—don't go totally extinct for all of eternity.

We want to snap that photograph of an orb or shadowy apparition, make a recording of the unheard answer to a question posed at an alleged haunted site, receive a tap on the shoulder or tug of a sleeve by some unseen hand, or experience some fleeting wispy vision of a known-dead human.

Some researchers gather thousands of stories for analysis in the hope of finding patterns or repetitive events to indicate some sort of intelligent remnant of a once living human who is now deceased.

All these are efforts to convince us that death is not a door closing, but a door opening to a new existence.

The ultimate experience, of course, would be that one of the researchers, familiar with the field, should die and contact the rest of us with information about the afterlife. Or with at least some indication that there is *some* kind of afterlife that awaits instead of the total silence of the grave.

No one in the field, not surprisingly, has volunteered for that duty of dying then attempting to contact us afterwards.

But it seems that someone highly esteemed in the ghost research field has delivered some proof of her continued existence.

All of us fortunate enough to know her and call her a colleague will never forget Rosemary Ellen Guiley. Extraordinarily intelligent, a remarkable researcher with unbounded curiosity and the ability to express her conclusions clearly and succinctly, whether speaking or writing, she was one of the best. She authored over sixty-five books—including 9 massive encyclopedias, which she called her "doorstops"—on paranormal phenomena such as witches, warlocks, demons, angels, fairies, ghosts and spirits, saints, intuition, scrying, vampires, reincarnation, dreams, UFOs, timeslips, tarot, mythical creatures and communication with the dead.

She also knew and had worked with many of the greats in the field like George Noory of *Coast-to-Coast AM*, Raymond Moody, author and researcher of after death studies, and Raymond Buckland, the author of the *Book of Spirit Communications* and some thirty other publications.

She and her husband Joe visited Carol and me many times and stayed with us in our home in Maryland and apartment in Gettysburg. Over wine and dinner, we discussed esoteric topics and had lots of laughs, many on ourselves.

Sadly, Rosemary's earthly life ended on July 18, 2019, and abruptly our wonderful discussions ended.

Or did they?

You would think with that kind of interest in the paranormal and its subtopic of life after death, that if there were some existence after life, someone interested enough in the topic to write scores of books on it and spend three decades of her life studying it full-time would want to try and let us know that she was right, that all of us in the field are correct, that there is indeed life that goes on after we "shuffle off this mortal coil."

Apparently, one night, she did.

One late summer evening a few months after Rosemary died, Carol and I were winding down our day out on the screened-in porch overlooking Dark Head Creek where we live. Carol's phone rang and it was Laine Crosby, one of the mediums we work with and author of several books on mediumship.

I suppose most people would be surprised at the information Laine passed on that night.

"I just heard from Rosemary," she said to Carol.

"What did she say?"

"She said to tell Joe that his new shoes—his wingtips—were in the closet."

They talked for a few more minutes then hung up.

"Maybe we should call Joe and pass it on," I said. "Wouldn't it be interesting if he'd been looking for his shoes and Rosemary decided to let him know where they were?"

So, Carol called Joe and told him what had just transpired. I have to admit that I was a little disappointed when he said that he already knew where his shoes were, overlooking the fact that we just had confirmation that Rosemary was communicating with us. Then came the twist.

"Yeah," Joe said. "Those were the shoes I bought for her funeral."

In other words, Rosemary saw the shoes Joe bought *after* she had died.

Our dear friend imparted such incredible information—that she was still watching—so matter-of-factly, as if we, as true paranormal investigators, shouldn't be amazed that she told us she had seen Joe put his new shoes away after she had transitioned.

I cannot say "after she died" unless you agree with my definition that death is an opening door and not a closing one.

In my youth, when I worked for the National Park Service at Gettysburg, I saw a lot of good friends move on to other parks. As they were leaving, they would always say that in the small branch of the government that was the National Park Service, you never said "Good-bye." It was always, "See you later."

Perhaps it's the same in this small branch of existence we call life.

If so, then, see you later, Ro.

A HAUNTED HIGHWAY

*"What happened in Gettysburg
Stayed in Gettysburg."*

—Mark Nesbitt

In 1963—one hundred years after the momentous battle—modern Route 15 was built for traffic to bypass Gettysburg in a wide half-circle to the east, down to the Pennsylvania-Maryland Line—the old "Mason and Dixon's Line." Gettysburg, like the hub of a multi-spoked wheel, can be reached by any one of six exits off the Route 15 bypass. After the southernmost exit, the Emmitsburg Road, one drives only a few miles, then leaves Pennsylvania and enters Maryland.

During the time of the Campaign and Battle of Gettysburg the direct routes from Gettysburg south into Maryland were the Emmitsburg Road, the Taneytown Road and the Baltimore Pike. All three, plus the Hanover Road, were approach routes to Gettysburg used by the Union Army once the battle commenced. In case of a catastrophic defeat for the Union Army at Gettysburg, they were also considered the direct retreat routes back to Washington.

Retreat routes for the Confederates would have been to the west toward the Shenandoah Valley—along the Fairfield Road and the Chambersburg Road—so that they could utilize the great wall of mountains bordering the eastern side of the Valley—like they did on their way north—to hide themselves from snooping Union cavalry. All they had to do was place small groups of soldiers to clog up the roads through the passes in the mountains to hold off prying northern eyes.

I have often wondered about the long trains of wounded drawn off the battlefield to be evacuated either to the Shenandoah Valley—for the Confederates—or south to Washington—for the Union wounded. How many of the sufferers died in the wagons, their bodies laid by the side of the road to be buried by the farmer who suddenly became undertaker for some mother's beloved son or a dear husband who ended up an unidentified corpse lying in the farmer's front yard. They were buried under some tree or near some particular rock in a field, and as the grass grew and years of grazing livestock knocked down whatever crude wooden headboard the farmer had supplied, they vanished from earthly memory, recalled in ancient rosters as only, "missing."

All along roads toward the Shenandoah Valley and toward Washington, the scene was replayed over and over, and now forgotten. So it was along the road to Emmitsburg.

I couldn't find the Halloween newspaper article where I'd first read the story of the Confederate ghost at Mount St. Mary's College in Emmitsburg, but I remember the story well enough to relate it here. How much of it was fabricated by the correspondent who first collected it can only be speculated—it happens, believe it or not.

But the story, as I recall it, begins with youthful romance: a young man and woman from Dixie fell in love under the southern stars. The war broke out and, moved by patriotism for his new country, he enlisted. Time was short before he was to leave, but he was sure the war would last only a few weeks before he and his Confederate comrades whipped the Yankees and would be home. He asked if she would wait for him to return; then they would be married and together forever. She pointed up to the stars. "As long as you can see those stars, I will wait for you, I will love you."

But war is the cruelest device ever to curse humankind. The short war turned into months and then years and many horrifying battles, each one playing the weird game of chance that war is, with some otherworldly Croupier making the decisions as to who will die and who will live. Finally, at Gettysburg, the young man was wounded. Since he ended up in Emmitsburg, he may have been with J. E. B. Stuart's cavalry, since Stuart's battalions passed through the area after the battle. Somehow, the young man was left in the town to die. The records show that dying men make strange requests. One of the last things he begged of his caretakers was to make sure he was buried with his face to the stars.

But some confusion occurred after he died. His body was suddenly abandoned and his request was lost. In their haste, whoever it was that was burdened with his (and perhaps many others') burials, possibly because of the hot July weather, made quick work of the interment. He was thrown into a nearby abandoned well and landed face-down.

And so, that may explain why, over the years, as present-day students of the college walk past where the abandoned well once stood, they are suddenly distracted by a disembodied voice with a distinct southern drawl, pleading uncomfortably close to their ears, "Roll me over."

Emmitsburg and the modern Route 15 bypass also bring to mind a story I heard, probably in my earliest days as a Park Ranger, about strange marks on the road, just a little south of the Pennsylvania-Maryland border. Moreso than any other spot on the highway, brake-marks of trucks and cars attempting an emergency stop have shown up. If memory serves correctly, the rubber tire marks were said to indicate where drivers have seen misty figures, dressed in uniforms of a long-past era, crossing or sometimes standing in the modern highway before them.

I had all but forgotten the story until Spring 2012. Carol, my wife, and I were attending a fundraiser for Susquehanna Service Dogs, an organization that breeds, raises, and trains dogs to help needful individuals, and for which we are volunteer "puppy-raisers."

A gentleman came up to my table upon which I was displaying my *Ghosts of Gettysburg* books and asked me if

I'd ever heard about the truck skid marks at the first exit on Route 15 across the Pennsylvania state line. He said he was a truck driver and had seen them many times. I recalled that I had heard such stories years before and said yes. He recounted the story of how drivers have applied the brakes and skidded to avoid a Confederate soldier in the road. He told me that he had stopped the past winter because a truck had skidded off the road into the median. He was talking to the state policeman at the scene who said that the driver had skidded to avoid a guy dressed in a Confederate uniform in the middle of the road. He mentioned to the trooper how unlikely it was for a reenactor to be out in the winter. He said the trooper nodded as if he knew what that meant.

Gleaning my files, as I always do, for material I have missed or wasn't able to use in previous books, I came across two e-mails sent to me years ago. One e-mail recounted an event that occurred another ten years prior to its writing, and told a story about a woman and her father returning to Maryland from a nephew's birthday party in Gettysburg, the night before Halloween. Around 11:30 P.M. they were passing Catoctin Mountain National Park near Thurmont, Maryland, on Route 15, when all of a sudden, the road virtually disappeared in a thick bank of fog. She remembered that the night was clear with low humidity and the air was temperate. She could not smell any burning leaves and so ruled out smoke. The fog was so thick she could not see to drive and pulled over, hoping the fog would soon dissipate. It was then that they began to smell the acrid odor of black powder, the main propellant of firearms during the Civil War. Her father confirmed the sulfur smell, since he had fired Civil War era rifled muskets from his own collection.

As quickly as what they at first thought was "fog" enveloped them, what they then concluded was phantom "battle smoke," vanished. She wondered if there was any battle in that vicinity.

History would seem to bear her out.

During the Confederate retreat, while the main Confederate Army and the wagon train of wounded were plodding their way through Fairfield and Cashtown on July 5, after being seen by a Union signal officer in Emmitsburg at dawn, Confederate Cavalry under J. E. B. Stuart rode southward toward Frederick, stopping at Graceham, southeast of Thurmont, Maryland, to feed and water the horses. From there Stuart rode west, passing through the area where the Route 15 highway would one day pass, on his way through the Catoctin Mountains. While there was no battle where the woman and her father drove that night in the 20th century, a large column of Confederate Cavalry rode through the area in the previous century, on July 5, 1863.

As far as the distinct odor, anyone who has been to a reenactment (or who reenacts) can vouch for the unmistakable smell of rotten eggs—sulfur from black powder—that embeds itself in the clothing and is intensified when the clothing gets rained upon. Could the woman and her father have had the strange *double* paranormal experience of driving through the mysterious substance of "ectoplasm" (sometimes called "paranormal mist") as well as the olfactory experience of actually *smelling* the apparitions?

Excursionists along Route 15, a little closer to Gettysburg, have reported driving through unexplainable clouds of "fog" on nights when the atmospheric conditions didn't seem right for fog to form. It happened to me, as reported in a previous *Ghosts of Gettysburg* volume, on the Baltimore Pike coming home over Cemetery Hill. My van passed through, then was literally filled with some sort of impenetrable "smog," only to have it dissipate a few seconds later.

Sometimes it is not just fog motorists see. From my "Lost Files" rises a story in which a woman claims to have "hit," with her car, a soldier on the same stretch of the Baltimore Pike. She apparently drove right through the man. So certain was she that she had just run over a fellow human being, she pulled her car over to investigate. But no injured man was there; no body; no blood.

Finally, an e-mail sent to me several years ago and found in the "Lost Files" asked if I knew anything about a Civil War ghost on horseback who has been seen riding along Route 15, just near the Taneytown Road exit. It was a foggy night when the e-mail writer—a truck driver—saw the apparition just on the right side of the white line along the side of the road as he was headed north. Suddenly the interior of his truck got icy cold, so cold that he could see his breath inside the cab (reminiscent of my experience on the Baltimore Pike). Then, as he passed the horseman, the temperature suddenly rose again to normal. Since the mysterious event, he said he has spoken to other truckers and discovered that he was not the only one to see the out-of-time horseback rider. Some of his fellow truckers claimed they have seen him more than once.

So, although the modern Route 15 bypasses the town and most of the battlefield of Gettysburg, it hasn't been able to bypass the remnant energy left by raw, piqued human emotions of men teetering on the precipice of life and sudden death that permeated the area over a century-and-a-half ago.

SOUTH OF GETTYSBURG

So, stand by your glasses steady,
The World is a web of lies.
Here's to the dead already,
Hurrah for the next one who dies!

—Drinking song of the Lafayette Escadrille

Often overlooked, the largest of the two "Round Tops" at Gettysburg is an important part of the story of the battle and—to at least one historian—could have held the key to victory for the Confederates.

Of course, Little Round Top is the more well-known of these two terrain features of the Gettysburg Battlefield. In the Fall of 1862, its western face had been cleared of trees; because of that clearing, Little Round Top provided an unimpeded view of what was to become, by the next summer, the famed battlefield named after the nearby town of Gettysburg.

The smaller of the two hills would become the anchor-point for the extreme left flank of the entire Federal Army of the Potomac, and the scene of countless heroic actions by Confederates attempting to wrest it from the Federals and by Federals countering each Confederate attempt with equal heroics.

It would also become the focal-point for the film "Gettysburg," and a magnet for anyone visiting the Gettysburg Battlefield after the movie's release.

Despite the illustriousness of the site, why the fighting there mattered has been debated in recent decades.

Of course, some of those who actually fought there (and, not surprisingly, those who were simply *near* the fighting there) from *both* sides, claim that its loss to the Confederates would have changed the course of the battle—and perhaps even the war. Their righteous opinions as to its importance may have something to do with their stories to friends and family during the post-war years of their participation in the great battle.

Their argument, fundamentally, is that Confederate artillery on the summit of Little Round Top would have enfiladed the rest of the Union line. In other words, enemy artillery could have fired down *along* the Union battle line on Cemetery Ridge. I, as a young Park Ranger, while giving scheduled history talks to visitors at the site and taking the surviving veterans' testimonies as knowledgeable and unimpeachable, espoused this view as part of a larger vision.

The problem with this model of the tactical importance of the terrain feature is that Little Round Top is anything but round: the summit is an oval running north and south, therefore cannons cannot be placed so that more than one or two at a time could fire down the Union line. And those hypothetical guns would be easily silenced by Union guns bringing converging fire to bear upon them.

The advantage I saw in the Confederates seizing Little Round Top, was not so much it being an artillery position, but in the fact that that their army had already captured the Emmitsburg Road to the west; holding Little Round Top with infantry then stretching their line to the east a few hundred yards would have had them capture the Taneytown Road. Both roads were vital for retreat in the event things went sour for the Union Army. Later, on July 2, Confederates attacking Culp's Hill came within a whisker of capturing the Baltimore Pike, the final retreat route for the Federals, making the cutting of the Taneytown Road retreat route even more important by placing the Southerners between nearly the entire Union Army and their capital, Washington. All of this, of course, is speculation and would have been subject to the whim of whatever mysterious Fates decide battles.

The interesting thing is that Big Round Top, in military terms, "commands" Little Round Top. Troops at the crest of Big Round Top could fire down upon Little Round Top making it untenable as a military position. And Confederates, at one point during the battle, actually captured Big Round Top.

Like so many events in war, it was totally by accident and only lasted a few minutes. During their march toward the Union left flank, half of Law's Confederate Brigade split off to attack toward Devil's Den. The two regiments remaining on the right of the brigade—the 15th Alabama and the 47th Alabama—continued in a straight line up the southern slope of Big Round Top to the summit of the highest point on the battlefield, driving off Union troops occupying it.

Why then, one must ask, with control of the commanding heights overlooking the battlefield, didn't the Confederates win?

First, while Little Round Top was cleared before the battle, Big Round Top remained wooded. Soldiers at the summit could barely see Little Round Top and the rest of the battlefield let alone target it with artillery or even infantry weapons.

Secondly, Lt. Colonel William C. Oates who commanded the 15th Alabama, was on the summit of Big Round Top as his men halted as a unit, exhausted from the climb up, the July heat, and the lack of water-filled canteens.

The story is famous Gettysburg lore: before the 15th began its march across the Plum Run valley and up the slope of Big Round Top, twenty-two members of the regiment were sent to fill the men's canteens, but failed to return with the water before the step-off.

As the de-hydrated men rested at the summit, a staff officer rode into the welter of sweating, thirsty soldiers and reminded Oates of his orders to move on, find and attack the enemy's flank post-haste. (I would have liked to have heard the enlisted men's comments at this point!)

Oates, at least according to his post-war memoirs, argued with the staff officer (Captain Terrell, of General Law's staff) that Big Round Top commanded the smaller hill and that his men could make it a veritable Gibraltar within a half hour. At least one historian, Glenn Tucker in *High Tide at Gettysburg*, agreed and would have liked to see what a regiment of Alabamians with axes could clear for a field of fire on Big Round Top. There was only one problem with that idea: the manpower was there, but not the axes.

The time it would have taken to send back to the main army, contact the engineers, gather together a couple hundred axes, and deliver them to the summit of Big Round Top, would have squandered any advantage clearing a field of fire would have gained.

So, orders remained orders. The parched Alabamians rose, aligned their ranks, and descended the slope of Big Round Top to meet the men of Colonel Joshua Chamberlain's 20th Maine…and glory.

The next day, July 3, the area just to the west of Big Round Top would become a whirling cyclone of battle involving cavalry charging into terrain where no mounted troops should have gone…a battle brought on more by vanity than practical tactics.

It was around 5:00 P.M. on July 3. Brigadier General Hugh Judson Kilpatrick and one of his brigade commanders, Brigadier General Elon J. Farnsworth, were overlooking the southern end of the battlefield. They could see in the distance, across the valley before them, some farmhouses, patches of timber, wooden fences and scores of large boulders strewn about the fields. Suddenly, down the ridge galloped a rider at full speed shouting, "We turned the charge; nine acres of prisoners!"

The charge he was shouting about—and grossly overstating— was Pickett's Charge, the climax of the infantry battles at Gettysburg. Kilpatrick had his orders to press and threaten the enemy and strike at an opportune moment should it come. Fighting between Union Cavalry and Confederate Infantry had already taken place near the Emmitsburg Road. Kilpatrick may have reasoned that, if the Confederates had been repulsed by the center of the Federal Army, his cavalry was in a perfect position to ride northward into the defeated column's flank, put them on the run, and achieve the decisive victory everyone had been hoping for since the war began.

He turned to young Farnsworth, just four days earlier a captain, now a brigadier general, advanced by the sometimes strange fortunes of war, and ordered him to take his cavalry brigade and charge.

Farnsworth was incredulous. He had to wonder if his commander was seeing the same terrain he was: the valley before them was boulder-strewn, half woodlots, and crisscrossed with the ubiquitous, solid stone walls and split-rail fences constructed by the Pennsylvania farmers. "General," he said. "Do you mean it? Shall I throw my handful of men over rough ground, through timber, against a brigade of infantry? The 1st Vermont has already been fought half to pieces; these are too good men to kill."

Kilpatrick had once expressed the notion—typically more bragging than reality—that cavalry could fight anywhere but at sea. "Do you refuse to obey my orders?" Kilpatrick said, in a not-so-veiled—and certainly premature—reference to insubordination. Then he added an unwarranted challenge, abhorrent to any military man: "If you are afraid to lead this charge, I will lead it."

Farnsworth, stung by Kilpatrick's raw attack on his manhood, stood in his stirrups. "Take that back!" More words were exchanged referencing, no doubt, personal courage and the foolish rashness of ordering a mounted charge into unsuited terrain. Kilpatrick finally withdrew. "I did not mean it; forget it." It was too late. Farnsworth said, "General, if you order the charge, I will lead it, but you must take the responsibility."

Another exchange between the two was unheard by witnesses, but Farnsworth rode away saying, "I will obey your order." Kilpatrick replied curtly, "I will take the responsibility."

After the 1st West Virginia had already been repulsed, Farnsworth took position at the front of the 1st Vermont Cavalry. The twenty-four-year-old, newly-minted general and his 300 men made the charge over ground totally unsuitable for cavalry action. Some of the survivors reported stone walls behind which Texans and Alabamians faced them were so high they could not have been breached without dismounting and throwing them down, stone by stone.

The ground was (and still is) an ankle-twisting, leg-breaking, rock and boulder covered tangle. Farnsworth's three battalions ended up riding in a huge circle behind the Confederate lines. An Alabama regiment turned around and poured fire into the element Farnsworth rode with. Farnsworth had his horse shot out from under him, borrowed a mount from an enlisted man, and doubled back. According to one account, Confederate sharpshooters appeared in the rocks above the charging column and poured fire into them. Farnsworth's men found their column split, charging together on either side of a rock wall, hemmed in by the wall and Confederate infantry on their other side. Farnsworth himself and his men plunged into an area where the rock wall narrowed toward the enemy line.

His troopers on the other side of the wall fought their way through the 15th Alabama, aided by the fact that the Alabama infantry was in the process of maneuvering around to meet them. Farnsworth and one of his officers, a Captain Cushman, went down together in the melee.

Field of Farnsworth's Charge

Confederates claimed that Farnsworth fought to the death with his pistol, then shot himself in the head to avoid the disgrace of being captured. Surgeons who found and examined his body found no bullet wound to the head. Five other enemy bullet wounds, found by the surgeons, precluded a self-inflicted *coup de grace* by Farnsworth. Confederates claimed he wore a white coat during the battle. Indeed, an officer with a terrible wound to the face was found insensible but alive by the surgeons. It was Captain Cushman who had been given a white coat by a female admirer who made it with her own hands and said—like a medieval lady sending her knight into battle (remember it was the Victorian Era)—that the coat would be impenetrable to enemy bullets. Farnsworth, so recently made a general, was wearing the blue officer's coat of General Alfred Pleasonton, given to him by his commander upon his advance in rank, an honor he'd had only four days to enjoy.

Of the 300 cavalrymen who started the charge, 65 never made it back, having fallen in the shadow of Big Round Top.

From the "locals" I met during my time there, growing up in a place like Gettysburg is a unique experience. Whether they live within the Borough of Gettysburg itself, or on one of the farms that surround the town, children grow up with the joys of small-town country life. A college, a seminary, and one of the most famous battlefields in the world lend an aura of sophistication to the town and provide sources for entertainment, knowledge and outdoor recreation. After they leave the area, they discover that, no matter where they go in the world, people have heard of their home town. Gettysburg is, as their motto states, "The most famous small town in America."

A long-time friend of mine and some of her friends were visiting Big Round Top. Having grown up in Gettysburg, it was not her first time to the large, historic hill. "Been there tons of times by myself to the top with the dogs or with friends sitting around."

The day started off just like that. She and several friends were on Big Round Top, sitting, enjoying the scenery and terrain of a part of the Gettysburg Battlefield not too many visitors bother to see. They were taking a break from the strenuous climb up, enjoying the peace and serenity the soldiers of a century-and-a-half before never knew, when suddenly, out of the thick woods came what she described as "a horrifying, blood-curdling scream," more terrible because of the nature of the history of the site juxtaposed with the current peaceful setting. Their conversation froze in mid-sentence as they all looked around at each other, realizing that each of them had heard it. After a few seconds there was a brief discussion as to what kind of animal could have made that sound. They came to the conclusion that only one kind of animal was capable of that dreadful scream: a human, and one with the realization that they were only seconds from their own extinction.

Stairs to Big Round Top Trail
Photo Courtesy of Maddy Butcher

She also told the story of sort of a treasure trove some of her friends found on Big Round Top. The story was told not on site or before a campfire on a proverbial "dark and stormy night," which, to her, would negate the main reason to tell the story—to scare the be-jeebers out of the females listening.

A schoolmate of hers, who was a reenactor, and some of his reenactor friends told her of a walk they had on Big Round Top. They had wandered off the pathway that leads to the top. They claim to have stumbled across a cave, smallish in size, perhaps nothing more than a large hole in the rocks, which expanded once underground—but large enough to attract their interest. As they peered inside the crevice, they were amazed to see piles of ammunition and stacks of weapons. In her letter, she doesn't say from what era the artifacts came, but it is doubtful that some modern hunter would stockpile ammo and guns in a damp cave for some future illegal hunt on National Park property. The impression she left in her letter was that it was a hiding place for soldiers, perhaps from a long-gone era, to store weapons for a later return.

There was so much in the cave that they realized they were going to have to get one of the guys' pickup trucks to haul it all. Not to mention some protective clothing, for this "cave" sounds just like the perfect den for copperheads, for which Big Round Top (and occasionally Little Round Top) are known.

When they came back with the truck and parked it in the lot, they went right to the spot where they'd been just an hour or so before, but were dumbfounded. Search as they might, up and down the slope, around the perimeter of the massive hill, they could not find the cave again. They left Big Round Top pondering: had it really been there or was it a mass hallucination? Or, as any good paranormalist might opine, was it one of those pesky "warps," or possibly a portal, through which they witnessed a vision of the past?

There have been stories circulating through the years of at least one disabled cannon, dumped into a local Gettysburg well, to keep it from falling into the hands of the enemy. It would be worth a pretty penny…if only you could locate the one well out of several hundred that dotted the battle-tortured countryside in and around Gettysburg. Not to mention all those wells that have gone dry and were filled in since the battle. Good luck.

A friend of mine lived in a cottage apartment complex near the south end of the battlefield just past the Round Tops. Once again, because the National Park doesn't own the property, it has been built up with modern businesses and many of the monuments to the cavalry units that fought in the vicinity are overlooked.

One day, however, she began to relate some of the things that were happening in her apartment. She felt that two spirits were predominant there. One was a deceased female relative; the other she called "The Captain." Noises seemed to be the hallmark of one or both of the ghosts, commotion that would be classified as "poltergeist activity" by paranormalists. The sounds of pots and pans moving around at 4:30 in the morning she attributed to the female spirit; rapping in the walls and other places later in the morning she blamed on "The Captain." One day, while doing chores around her place, she felt the Captain's presence.

But it was one evening when she left a tape recorder on overnight that disturbed her the most. Playing it back the next morning, she got the distinct sounds of footsteps wandering around her apartment and the unmistakable noise of the drawers opening and closing—all going on while she slept. Most disturbing was the other sound, soft thudding, rhythmic in nature, like something out of an Edgar Alan Poe story of psychological horror: the phantom echo of a human heartbeat.

In my years as a Park Ranger at Gettysburg, I had many unforgettable experiences, my favorite being the opportunity to interact with the visitors, telling them the documented stories of unbelievable heroism and deeds accomplished by the soldiers who fought in the battle and the men and women of the town who endured. Beyond that, perhaps my next best experiences were with the people I met at work: professional historians at the park, and from the town.

One historian I, and many other students of the battle are indebted to, is Gregory Coco author of some 16 books and a dozen scholarly articles about Gettysburg and the Civil War. *A Strange and Blighted Land: Gettysburg: The Aftermath of a Battle*, was voted number 12 of the top 50 books on the Civil War ever written. Another received an award from Eastern

National Parks and Monuments Association—a former book clearinghouse and purchaser for the National Park Service.

He was a Park Ranger in the Interpretive Division of the National Park and a Licensed Battlefield Guide, both of which demand a vast knowledge of the battle. Prior to his employment at the Park, he had been in Law Enforcement as a Louisiana State Trooper and Lafayette City Police officer. He was also a Vietnam veteran, receiving the Bronze Star, Purple Heart, Combat Infantry Badge, Good Conduct Medal and Vietnam Campaign Medal.

Greg—or "Coke" to his friends—was born in Louisiana and his southern-leaning roots are evident in his books, many about the forgotten southerners who suffered wounds in combat and subsequently died far from their homes or were killed in battle, then were subsequently "lost," buried in an unmarked and now forgotten grave where they remain to this day. Visitors would often ask us about the dead: "Did they get them all, or are some still buried on the battlefield?" to which we were told to answer, they got them all, perhaps to discourage attempts at finding any still buried. In his book Wasted Valor: The Confederate Dead at Gettysburg, Greg was apparently tired of the obfuscation and, after some calculations, determined that as many as 1,500 individual Confederates may remain buried on the battlefield.

Greg was also continually teasing me about my ghost books. I have no doubt he respected my writing and researching—I would have heard about it if he hadn't. It was the fact I advocated that there was something that went on after this terrestrial life, that there was a mystical spirit, a transcendent soul that moved on to another realm, his experiences in law enforcement and Vietnam had convinced him otherwise. I took the teasing in the way it was meant—good-naturedly—from Greg.

Reviewing his books for this chapter, I ran across another account, besides the one I had from near the Rose Farm, of glowing graves that convinced the wartime witness that souls were rising to heaven before his eyes. This one occurred, appropriate to this chapter, on or near Big Round Top. A citizen of Gettysburg who was visiting a relative in the area also saw, emanating from the shallow graves on July 7, a "phosphorescent light," after dark, strikingly strange enough to record in his remembrances.

I ran across a copy of an interview Greg had written up about a farmhouse owned during the battle by the Beamer Family, located near Big Round Top, that was, in Greg's handwriting, the "scene of Farnsworth's Charge." He recorded that the then-occupants of the house had been hearing "ghostly noises" and experiencing "other mysterious happenings since they moved in." They had recently done some renovations inside the house; after those, the activity increased. (This, of course, is typical in many older, haunted houses, as if the spirits, settled in their surroundings, become agitated that their status quo is being interrupted.)

Some of the original construction is log and retains bullets from the battle. During Farnsworth's action, 1st Vermont Cavalryman Rufus D. Thompson, Company L, was wounded and brought to the house where he died on July 6. He was buried in the yard. A check of the website Find a Grave indicates he was from Colchester, Vermont, and was 20 years and 8 months old when he died. The site also shows a picture of his cenotaph—a marker where there is no body—in Champlain Cemetery, Colchester, Chittenden County, Vermont.

Knowing Greg had no interest in ghosts, I can't help but think that he jotted some of the notes down not for himself, but for someone who might be interested in ghost stories of the battlefield. Somehow, they got to the right person.

WALKING SHADOWS

The empty silent house was not vacant at all
But filled with presences like held breath....

—William Faulkner, *The Reivers*

I was autographing my books one evening at the *Ghosts of Gettysburg Tour Headquarters* when a man came in and introduced himself.

I recognized the last name—Nett—as a famous one throughout Gettysburg. A relative of his was a park ranger I had worked with in his last years with the park. As a matter of fact, we drank a few beers at his house on Hospital Road. I had also shared a few beers with the man's cousin. His visit that night at the tour headquarters, however, was not to invite me out for a couple of cold ones. It was far more serious and personal.

He told me that growing up in his family's farmhouse on Sachs Road to the east of Little Round Top—bloody territory if there ever was any—he and his family had been disturbed more than once by unexplainable occurrences that seemed to indicate that his boyhood home was more than the safe space it appeared to others, but indeed may have been haunted.

As the battles of July 2, 1863, raged west of Little Round Top, this area became the refuge and dying ground for the wounded whose torn bodies and limbs literally watered the earth with blood around the Nett's farm.

Not surprisingly, the old farmhouse and barn—like most large structures behind the battlelines of 1863—were used as a hospital during and after the Battle of Gettysburg. This farm was particularly cursed by the battle since the fighting for Little Round Top, Devil's Den, the Triangular Field and the Wheatfield were areas of particularly savage combat providing wounded copiously to that area behind the lines. This means that activity—the comings and goings of nurses, surgeons, orderlies, the wounded, the dying and removal of the dead—was at a peak from shortly after the battle started until the scattered hospital sites began to be consolidated at Camp Letterman when it opened on July 20, 1863.

In other words, human emotional energy was running at an all-time high level during that period and may have left its apparently indelible, sometimes not-so-subtle, mark upon all things there—land, barn, out-buildings, farmhouse and, of course, the modern-day inhabitants.

He was kind enough to send me a multi-paged collection of his experiences growing up in the house. His memories give an insight into what it is like to live in a farmhouse on one of the most famous and bloody battlefields in history.

The first event he remembers took place when he was only seven or eight years old. At the time, the house did not have central air conditioning. Windows were opened in the summer. His room had two double windows to allow the breeze off the former fields of battle to blow through the house. Lying awake one night, he was gazing out the window, when he saw the distinct silhouette of the muzzle of a musket with a bayonet attached pass into then out of his view, as if a soldier from a century past was marching by.

Terrified, he let out a scream, which brought his mother into the room. His cry was so filled with fear his older sister was awakened and ran into the room as well. While her presence was comforting, it also meant that it wasn't her playing a trick to frighten him. Casting about for a logical explanation to calm her child, his mother suggested that perhaps it was just a cat that passed by the window. But even at eight years old he knew that the small brick ledge outside of the window would have placed the animal so close to him that he surely would have recognized it.

Several years passed, but as if to remind him that the spirits were still there and had all the time in the world to remind the living of that fact, they gave another, more intimate example of their presence. He was, he recalled, thirteen or fourteen years old. It was again late at night and he was in bed. He was awakened by the obvious feeling of someone sitting down on the end of his bed: the bed depressed and there was that feeling of the sheets tightening around his feet. Too frightened to roll over, he lay there, trying to forget the feeling of having his personal space violated by someone from a previous century, now perhaps invisible, who had long ago left the realm of the living. Much later, exhaustion finally returned him to sleep.

The next frightening, unexplainable experience occurred in 1990 or 1991—coincidentally, and to show there was no suggestive influence, that was before the *Ghosts of Gettysburg* books were published—when his mother purchased a wind-up swing chair for his baby nephew to keep at their house for when his sister visited with her child. It stayed in his parents' living room most of the time. In this case, everyone in the family was out of the room. Suddenly, from down the hall, they heard a strange noise. When they went into the living room to investigate the sound, the baby-chair was swinging as fast as it could possibly go. Each looked around at the others; questions were asked if anyone had touched the swing or wound it up. Their answers made the event inexplicable and even more frightening: No one had been in the room or anywhere near the swing.

When confronted with the supernatural, many people wonder why they, in particular, were singled out for an experience. It is often those experiences that convince a person that they may be overly-sensitive to the goings-on of the Other World. Paranormalists have classified some of these sensitivities, which may come singly or as a package. There are those who experience Clairvoyance— "clear-seeing," the ability to actually see spirits. Some hear echoes from the Next World. They are deemed Clairaudient. Some report being touched: having a tactile experience. Others report getting unusual, unexplainable "feelings." They are sometimes classified as "sensitives."

Many, if not most of us, at one time used to be sensitive to the supernatural. Children often have "imaginary friends", playmates to whom the children speak and interact who are utterly invisible to their parents. As soon as the children begin to attend school, parents tend to talk their kids out of mentioning their "friends" that only they can see—giving the excuse that the "friend" is only a figment of their imagination. The memory of the imaginary friend fades, until one day the child—now an adult—will come across an old photo from the family album and recognize the face of their childhood "imaginary" friend with whom they used to play and communicate. It turns out that the picture is of their own great-grandparent as a child. That's only one example of childhood sensitivity.

The reason the man as a youth experienced paranormal events was explained later in life.

Shortly after graduating from Gettysburg High School, the man attended visual arts school and set up a home studio in the family room in the basement of the old farmhouse. Deep into an assignment one night he suddenly got the feeling that he was being watched. Soon after, he got the feeling that the "entity" had moved from his one side to the other as if watching what he was working on. He fought the urge to leave his work for the safety of the upstairs and managed to finish his assignment. Later, after learning more about the paranormal and "false positives," he tried to rationalize that, because the wiring for the house went through the basement, he may have been the unwitting victim of high electromagnetic fields from the house wiring in the area.

High electromagnetism has indeed been shown in some cases to influence the mind into experiencing what appear as "ghostly" events. It would be more understandable as a cause if the house wasn't located where it was—so near one of the bloodiest battlefields in history. However, it does show that the man was attempting to explain his experiences in a skeptical, rational way.

One final personal experience had occurred when he was in his mid-twenties in the front yard of the house, where there was a decorative, old-fashioned, hand-operated well-pump.

Historically, after the Battle of Gettysburg began, the soldiers, after their long, forced marches on those hot, mid-summer days, swarmed farmhouse wells refilling their dry canteens. And when those farmhouses later became makeshift hospitals, the wells were nearly always pumped dry for quenching the never-ending thirst of the wounded. The well pumps were worked incessantly for several days.

He was with two other relatives and it was a hot July day. He remembered glancing over to see the pump handle being in the down position as they walked past it toward the front porch. The smaller family member began playing near the porch when suddenly, all three heard the distinct sound of the cast-iron handle slamming down. Within a few seconds, in spite of the hot July day, the other family members felt a sudden icy chill embrace them. As if the pump was again the most sought-after spot on the farm in July, did the now spectral remnants of parched soldiers once more gather to slake an eternal thirst?

His father worked for the Pennsylvania Game Commission and would often come home late into the night after patrolling during hunting seasons. One night the young man's mother was awakened by someone walking to the kitchen down the hall. She heard the faucet turn on and off as if someone were getting a drink of water. She assumed it was her husband who had come home after work, but no one came back to bed. She got out of bed and walked down the hall, into the kitchen and living room, but couldn't find anyone. She saw that her son was still asleep and knew that her daughter was now living in her own home married with her own children. No rational, earthly explanation for the footsteps of an apparently thirsty phantom was ever discovered.

One day, after his father had retired, the young man was in the house awaiting a repairman. He had dozed off in the living room. He was awakened by what sounded like the back door into the kitchen opening. Becoming fully awake, he heard a few footsteps, but no one came into the living room and he never heard the door close. He stood to go to the kitchen and greet the repairman, but no one was in the kitchen and the door was closed. He looked outside expecting to see the repair company's truck, but no vehicle was there.

His mother would experience sudden and random cold breezes throughout the house even though the installation of central air conditioning and closed windows would rule out any wind blowing through. Yet, no one else living in the house experienced the cold winds inside as she has.

The man has now identified what is known as poltergeist activity as becoming more and more common in the Civil War era farmhouse. "Poltergeist" of course, is often defined as "noisy ghost" and refers to an entity that turns lights on and off, rattles doors and door handles and moves items. Often the activity is more playful (and annoying) than dangerous. But sometimes their pranks can go a little too far.

His father was looking for the car keys, which were habitually kept in a drawer in an antique dry sink that was located in the kitchen. Unable to find them one day, he asked his wife if she had inadvertently placed them somewhere else. When she answered in the negative, he assumed he must have missed them and emptied the entire drawer out onto the kitchen table, but still could not find the keys. The spare car keys were located and used for several weeks until, one day, his father opened the drawer in the dry sink to see the original keys back where they had always been.

Things would continue to go missing for months or sometimes years before turning up again where they always had been kept. A stapler, a bunt-cake pan from his mother's kitchen, and a screwdriver from his father's tool belt are just a few of the items that have vanished only to reappear later.

A noted Gettysburg family, whose ancestors endured the battle of 1863, and its tragic aftermath of agony and uncertainty, has learned to live with the ghosts of the soldiers who once, for a few short weeks—that time as living beings—inhabited the farm they inherited.

THE GHOST HOUSE...AGAIN

Take courage mortal; death cannot banish you from the universe.

—Benjamin Franklin

It is often odd and unnerving to the living, that we now pass through the same space as the dead once did—and, perhaps, still do. Which may be why some people get a strange feeling when they enter the *Ghosts of Gettysburg Candlelight Walking Tours* Headquarters at 271 Baltimore Street in Gettysburg.

From what I have come to call my "Lost Files"—bundles of letters from years ago that turned up in a storage box recently—a woman wrote explaining a "strange" feeling she got when she walked through the doors of the Tour Headquarters to purchase tickets for one of our walking tours. It was 3:30 in the afternoon—certainly not anywhere near "The Witching Hour"—but she went on to explain that, although not psychic in the true sense of the word, she had realized that she was sensitive to the paranormal.

After buying her tickets, she said that it felt as if someone was physically pulling her to a door that led to some steps, a reference to the door that leads to the stairs to the private second floor. The energy from the entity was so strong that the woman began to visualize in her head a woman, middle-aged, holding a basket of flowers. She said that she felt that the woman ran the place and the other "beings" in the house.

The woman with the strong personality she described can be none-other than Mary Ann Kitzmiller.

The Kitzmiller family owned the house from just after the Civil War ended in 1866 until it was finally sold out of the family in 1924 after Mary died January 21, 1923 at age 86. She has been described by our mediums as a very head-strong, iron-willed woman, ahead of her times. It was Mary Ann Kitzmiller and her husband David who added, around 1888, to the original balconied section, the gabled Baltimore Street-facing part of the building. Over the years that I have owned the property, she has interacted with the living scores of times, usually expressing her opinion forcefully.

David Kitzmiller and Children
Photo Courtesy of Tim Smith and Adams County Historical Society

Just as it is a part of a living human's nature to get comfortable with one's surroundings, apparently, once in the spirit realm, the dead appear to like their surroundings to remain relatively unchanged. The fact that so many weird, unexplainable events were reported during house renovations at the Ghost Tour Headquarters—and other historic sites around the world—may tell us that we all—dead or alive—like our comfortable *status quo* unchanged.

The *Ghosts of Gettysburg Candlelight Walking Tours* has operated ghost tours from the building on the corner of Baltimore and Breckenridge Streets since 1997. In fact, since it was purchased, the house has been the subject of chapters in almost every *Ghosts of Gettysburg* volume. Unexplainable events have happened spontaneously in and around the house since the first investigation shortly after its purchase.

As the years passed, the house has been the venue for various paranormal investigations—several hundred, as a matter of fact—as the *Ghosts of Gettysburg* business conducted learning/investigation weekends, like "Mysterious Journeys Weekends," "Haunted Crime Scenes Weekends," and "Spirit Quest Weekends," for interested ghost hunters to learn additional investigating techniques.

Numerous private investigations have also been done by other reputable ghost hunting groups and stories from the house have been featured on numerous television programs, such as "Ghosts of Gettysburg, I & II," on *The History Channel* in 1994-5, "Mysterious Journeys," "My Ghost Story," "Kindred Spirits," with the most recent being "The UnXplained" with William Shatner. Stories from the house have been seen on the *Travel Channel*, *Discovery Channel* and *History Channel*.

The main section of the house was built in the 19th Century. While the gabled section fronting Baltimore Street was added on by the Kitzmiller family around 1888, the section with the balcony on the second-floor dates back to the battle era and into the 1830s and bears some bullet pock marks. We're pretty sure that the section with the balcony shows up under magnification in the famous photo of Abraham Lincoln riding in the procession to dedicate the National Cemetery, November 19, 1863.

There were several families associated with the house over the years. Jacob Heck shows up in the records as the original owner of a building on the property—a carriage trimmer's shop—probably in the footprint of the western-most section, likely built in 1834. The building was substantially enlarged in 1837 to the entire two-storied, balconied section.

The next owner was Andrew Woods, also a carriage trimmer. My research in 2008, led me to the conclusion that, while Andrew and Sarah Woods owned the house during the Battle of Gettysburg, he and his family were probably living in New Windsor, Maryland, and renting the house to a family named Young.

I mentioned my research to Carol, my wife. She called Julie, one of our medium friends, who was helping us out working at the Ghost House part-time and asked her, besides the "regular" ghosts in the house—The Hecks, the Woods, the Kitzmillers—was there anyone else Julie was picking up on?

I called Julie and hour or so later on a different matter. Before I could even mention it, Julie blurted out, "Young. That's the other name I think is associated with the house, but I don't know if I got that independently or because the last person who called to make a reservation was named Young." Slightly amazed (although *nothing* my psychic friends come up with anymore should amaze me), I told her that "Young" was the name of the family I thought had been living there at the time of the battle. Then, out of the blue, Julie asked if I was aware of any letters scratched in the cellar. I said no, but I had never looked. I asked where and she said in the northwest corner, which would be the oldest (the house has two) cellars. "W Y" were the letters she said

I'd find. Further research for this book may have revealed who the graffiti writer might be.

Jacob B. Young (1819-1897) had enlisted in Co F., 87th Pennsylvania Volunteer Infantry on September 25, 1861, while in his 40s. By April 10, 1862, he was discharged on a surgeon's certificate. (The 87th had many recruits from Gettysburg, including Jack Skelly, friend of Jennie Wade, a number of men from the Sheads family, Culps, and other names still associated with Gettysburg.) Jacob was married to Mary A. (Guinn) Young (unknown birth date-1898.) They had four children: Carrie Virginia Young (1846-1925), Louisa S. Young (1850-1916), Mary E. Young (1858-1941) and William Young (1863-1932). Could he be our "W Y?"

In 1938, Mary, the last surviving member of the family who lived in the house during the battle, was interviewed for a story that appeared in the Gettysburg Times. It may have been a part of the Great Depression's WPA's (Works Progress Administration) Writers' Project, a federal program that sent unemployed writers around the country to interview witnesses and record history, folklore, geography, architecture, and local travel information from American cities, big and small. Arguably, the most important of the histories were the slave narratives and recordings—testimonies and music documented from former slaves—but in an historic town like Gettysburg, any older citizen who had experienced the battle was worthy of an interview.

Mary E. Young was in her early eighties when she recounted her family's experiences during the tumultuous three-day Battle of Gettysburg. Of course, she was only five years old when the battle violently swirled about her house on Breckenridge Street, so some of what she "remembered" may have been other family members' experiences told to her as she grew up, because the article contains some blatant errors, some of which could be blamed on the writer as well.

For example, the headline mentions that Mary Young said her mother talked to General Reynolds just two hours before his death. An officer apparently rode up to her house on Breckenridge Street and told her to get her family into the cellar for their own safety. It was after he left that a soldier came up to her and asked her if she knew to whom she had been talking, to which she replied in the negative. The soldier identified him as General Reynolds. The rider was identified as a *southern* officer in the article. Of course, Major General John F. Reynolds, commander of the Union Army First Corps was a Federal (northern) officer. Someone (the soldier, the writer, Mrs. Young or whomever told her the story) misidentified the officer.

She also said that Jeb Stuart's cavalry came through Gettysburg in "two divisions" marching up Baltimore Street on June 26, 1863. She may have been referring to Major General Jubal Early's troops—infantry, not cavalry—who stopped in Gettysburg on June 26, 1863, to demand money, food and shoes on their way through as an advance force of Lee's main body of the army. Stuart, of course, was still in Virginia, on his way to ride around the Union Army.

But as far as events that occurred in her own neighborhood were concerned, her stories are pretty interesting.

Reading the article, we discover that after attempting to hide in the cellar, (two cellars still exist with one entry through the balcony porch and another through the west side of the foundation), she and her mother found it stifling in July and couldn't stay there even through the first day of the three-day battle and eventually went next door. Sometime on that first day of fighting, (most likely as wounded Union troops filtered back into Gettysburg from the battle north and west of town and before the Confederates captured Gettysburg) her family had hidden a Union soldier, wounded in the hand, in their attic. (The attic where he hid is still accessible from the second floor.)

When the Confederates took possession of the town, Mary Young told the writer that they also occupied her house, trapping the wounded Yankee hiding in the attic.

Somehow, Mary and her mother diverted the attention of the Confederate soldiers elsewhere and they managed to sneak the Union soldier out from under their noses and hustle him next door into the McCullough home, where he hid until the battle was over. They thus saved the man from a horrible stay in some deadly Confederate prison-pen; he left Gettysburg with his comrades on July 4.

Finally, we learn that on the morning of July 4, when Union soldiers re-captured the Breckenridge Street section of town, they discovered 25 rebels who had overslept in the barn owned by the Youngs, but used by neighbors for keeping their horses.

From sources such as Dr. Thomas A. Desjardin's maps, produced for the Friends of the National Parks at Gettysburg, we know which Confederate troops were located near the house on Breckenridge Street. Keep in mind that all maps show the units in a straight line, but the soldiers, when they weren't fighting, wandered from their positions to seek food and water. So, while the maps show specific units at specific streets a block or so from the house at 271 Baltimore Street, they were probably the soldiers who found refuge from the July sun in the house.

In the late afternoon of July 2, half a block south on the opposite side of Baltimore Street from the house, troops from Hays's Brigade are shown in a line running northeast in this order: 5th, 6th, 9th, 7th, and 8th Louisiana Regiments.

On July 3, they were pulled back to Middle Street northwest of the house. General John B. Gordon's Georgians (60th, 31st, 13th, 61st, 38th, 26th Georgia Regiments) occupied the lines near Hays's July 2 position, not quite to Baltimore Street, with their line ending just south of the German Reformed Church on Stratton and High Streets.

The 5th Alabama, in a spread-out skirmish line, was positioned generally along the east/west alley that runs south of 271 Breckenridge. Desjardin puts the line running through the 90 degree turn to the west behind the Historic Shriver House and Garlach properties.

Therefore, the closest troops (according to the maps) on July 2 would have been the 5th and 6th Louisiana Infantry.

On July 3, the 44th and 4th Georgia (Doles's Brigade) stationed on Long Lane two blocks west of the house would have been the next closest Georgia troops after Gordon's men.

Interestingly, years ago, several mediums who visited the house indicated the identity of the troops sheltering on the first floor as Georgia troops with one notable exception: "Hank," who at least three employees have literally "run into" in the Green Room on the first floor, was identified as coming from Louisiana, but was temporarily attached to these Georgia troops while in the house.

Mediums have named no other states represented in the house besides Georgia and Louisiana.

Needless to say, any of the other-worldly individuals or groups mentioned above could potentially reside permanently or temporarily in what we affectionately call "The Ghost House."

So, owning an historic house that has spawned ghost stories for going on three decades gives the owner an opportunity to do some experimentation in the field of the paranormal. It's like having a closed laboratory in which to study the Other World.

As I wrote in one of my first stories on the house, the first medium I invited in to tell me her impressions of the house was Karyol Kirkpatrick, who had often been on the Maury Povich Show and lived relatively locally. On her first walk-through of the house, she insisted that I would have evidence of the presence of child ghosts—balls bouncing, running footsteps with no visible source, and marbles rolling on the floor.

I've written about an employee, who was sensitive to the paranormal, who was working the front counter one night. No customers were in the office, the door to the upstairs was open and, probably since her mind was relaxed, she saw materialize at the base of the stairway, a boy whom she described as being 3-5 years old with dirty blonde hair, wearing a white shirt and trousers with suspenders. As suddenly as he entered this world, within seconds, he was gone.

Photo Courtesy of Jeff Ritzmann

Periodically, I will invite select paranormal teams, usually individuals whom I've known for a number of years, to investigate the house. One team, led by Jeff Ritzmann from Maryland, in an overnight investigation managed to capture in the house what is the very best photo of a spirit I have ever seen. It is of a little boy, appearing perhaps 3-5 years of age, with dark hair, wearing a white shirt with trousers and suspenders. It was published in *Ghosts of Gettysburg VII.* Later, a woman sent me a letter with the observation that she thought she saw in the picture that the little boy was holding hands with another child. Though it may be the product of pareidolia (the human brain making an image of matrixed input) *something* can be seen behind the child apparently touching his right hand.

Kayla Miner and her husband Eric have been living in the apartment above the headquarters office for several years. Kayla and her remarkable mediumistic gifts were featured in my book, *Gettysburg's Hidden Haunted Hotspots: Spirits, Apparitions and Haunted Places on and off the Battlefield* (Second Chance Publications, 2022).

In one investigation, without telling her where she was going, we took her to one of Gettysburg's Hospital Woods sites for the first time. I asked her if she was picking anything up. She said she was approached by two officers; that they were standing there, right in front of her. She said they had been wounded and were at the hospital. I asked her if they gave her their names and she said they did. Out of nearly 190,000 soldiers and support non-combatants who were at Gettysburg, what are the odds that she would guess, out of the blue, the names of two who were present, wounded and ended up at this particular Hospital Woods site out of several "hospital woods" located around the battlefield. She gave me two names, the state they came from, and the number of their regiment. After some searching, (which wouldn't have happened if she hadn't gotten all that information,) I found the names of the soldiers. It was a feat beyond chance or a lucky guess and it would have been impossible for her to research since she had no idea where we were going that day.

Living upstairs in the "Ghost House" has provided Kayla and Eric with some highly unusual experiences…virtually from their first night in the house. I'll quote from a "ghost diary," she's been keeping:

> "We would stay at the apartment on weekend getaways to Gettysburg. The first night staying here I was awoken at 2:30 A.M. by a little boy standing on my side of the bed staring at me. He had dirty blonde to light brown hair and blue eyes with knickers on. I told him he can't be doing that, and he just disappeared."

> "Another time we came to spend the weekend I kept getting woken up at 6 A.M. every morning. I looked at Eric and said I'm going downstairs to see who's making all the ruckus this early in the morning. I opened the door and walked back to the one room; there stood a man dressed in 1800 clothing. I said I'm trying to sleep! He looked at me and said yeah, well I have work to do. I said could you at least keep it down for another hour. He walked away from me. I haven't heard him making noise again."

Of course, over the decades numerous women have been associated with the house: Jacob Heck's wife, Sarah Woods, Mrs. Young and her daughters, and, of course, Mary Kitzmiller, who owned the house the longest. They all lived out their day-to-day lives here, watched loved ones born here, family members pass on here, and some died themselves within the walls of the house at 271 Baltimore Street. With so many passing through, it would be difficult to identify the mysterious woman Kayla and Eric keep running into while living in the house....

> "We were deep cleaning the apartment to get it ready for us to move in. I kept feeling like someone was peeking around the bathroom door as I was scrubbing the tub. I turned around and a short lady with brown hair peeked around the door. About 5 minutes later Eric was coming out of the upstairs office and asked

me where I was going. I turned around from scrubbing and said what are you talking about? He said wait?! I just saw you going down the steps! He realized he had just seen someone of the nonliving. That night I decided I was going to sleep in and take a break from deep cleaning. At least so I thought… I heard a woman's voice that morning say "Good Morning, It's 8 o'clock." I opened my eyes to see no one there, looked at my clock and it was indeed 8 A.M.

One morning I was waking up and smelled brownies baking. I went out to the kitchen thinking maybe Eric made brownies, only to realize he was still sleeping. The phantom smell went away as soon as I walked into the kitchen.

Eric would only be here on weekends when I first moved down here. He would leave Sunday afternoons before I went to work. I finished up with my workday and came back upstairs. Grabbed a quick dinner and sat down to work on my laptop. I heard a woman say where is Eric? I looked up and saw a shorter woman standing there with brown hair and a brown checker dress on. I answered her saying oh he had to get back to go to work. I continued working on my laptop for a few seconds before I realized wait, I'm the only one here. I looked back up and no one was standing there.

I wasn't feeling good one evening, so I went to bed early. Eric decided to go out in the living room and film for his YouTube channel. He was almost done when he thought he heard me walking by the bedroom door thinking I had to use the bathroom but didn't want to disturb him. He came to check on me only to realize I was sound asleep. He went back to filming and saw a shadow go across the living room."

"Hank," you will recall, was the Louisiana soldier apparently ordered to watch over the tired or wounded Georgians on the first floor of the building.

Our first knowledge of Hank's presence was when Katie, our daughter, came back to the Carriage House, at the back of the property, after she'd locked up the "Ghost House." She was shaking. She said she'd bumped into a large figure in the Green Room—had to walk *around* him as a matter of fact—to leave the building. Julie also saw him. Being ex-military, she recognized that he came to an *en garde* position with his musket, and assumed it was his duty to protect the wounded in the building. Both women said the figure was huge— "linebacker size." Again, from Kayla's ghostly events diary:

> "We were getting ready to film a commercial for the office. So, Eric went down to the green room to get set up and turn on the lights. As we always do, he said "Hello Hank." All of the sudden a large black mass appeared like it was going into guard mode. He said, "it's ok Hank, it's just me." The mass disappeared."

Kayla's experience one rainy day was reminiscent of the events that transpired during a rainy-night tour and documented in *Ghosts of Gettysburg VII.* One of our guides had a group of middle school children outside the Ghost House just as it began to rain. She took the children and chaperones onto the porch to get out of the weather. Though the office was closed and all the employees had left, our guide and her startled customers heard boots stomping through the downstairs. As they were trying to make sense of the non-sensical, the stomping stopped...then started again, but on the open balcony just above their heads. Back and forth the phantom boots went, not just annoying the guide and her customers, but convincing them that their fun ghost tour had turned into something terribly real. Kayla may have witnessed evidence of that same visitor:

"It was a rainy day. I swore I had seen someone peeking in my living room window. I thought maybe a friend had been seeing if I was home before they were going to knock. So, I opened the door to see who it was and there was absolutely no one on our balcony porch. I went out and sat on the chair afterwards to listen to the rain and looked over to my left and there was a dirty boot print right next to the chair. I, of course, snapped a picture of it. I went back in to grab something and came back out a few minutes later and the boot print was completely gone. Also, there were no other boot prints along the porch—just in that area that I saw someone looking into the living room window."

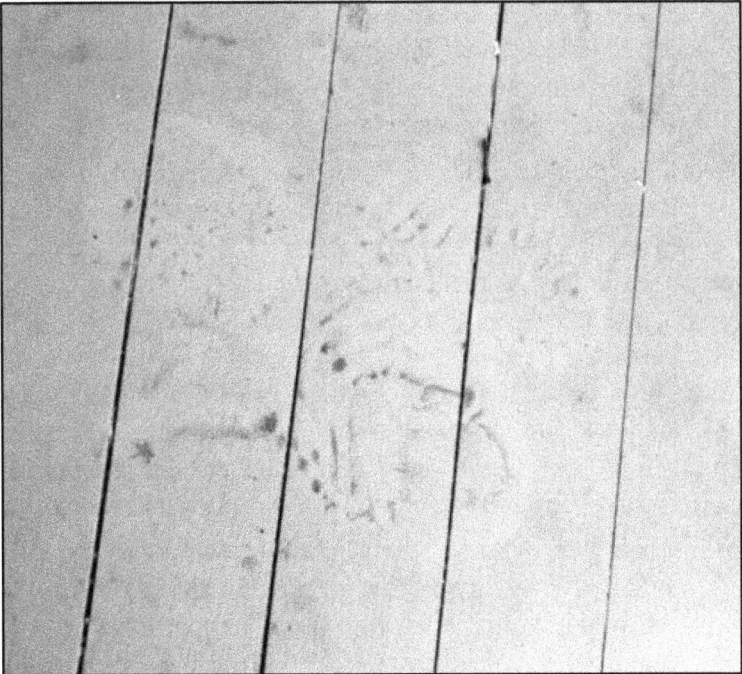

Boot Print Photo Courtesy of Kayla Miner

Animals are usually extremely sensitive to spirit energies. Some have theorized that it is because spirits register on detectors as electromagnetic energy, and animals, with all their fur, are more sensitive to that type of energy. One woman who was staying in the apartment above the Ghost Tour Headquarters, witnessed her own cat acting like she was playing with another invisible cat.

Kayla had a more vivid experience, though with her dog:

"I was working downstairs in the office and had my dog Diesel with me. After work we came back upstairs and as soon as he came through the door he started barking and growling while running to the bedroom. His hair was standing up and his teeth were showing. I, of course, took off after him to see what was going on. There stood a taller man with dark brown hair and black clothing. He was pale with dark circles around his eyes. He had a stern look on his face. I told him he needed to leave now and that he wasn't welcome here. He then turned to me, smiles as if he's saying I'll be seeing you again and then just vanished."

An animal reacting to what we perceive might be a paranormal event means that it is not an illusion or hallucination limited to the human imagination. Dogs, by instinct, alert to a perceived danger, something they actually see, never judging whether what they're seeing can or cannot be real.

There have been other auditory events as well. Kayla and Eric have heard the liquor bottles in Eric's bar clanking together when no one was near them, and one Halloween night (of course, *Halloween*), Kayla and another employee, Jeff, heard sounds that convinced her they needed to be checked out:

"Jeff and I were working together in the office on Halloween night when we kept hearing footsteps behind the door leading upstairs. He opened the door, and no one was there. He came back over and sat down we continued to talk when we heard the footsteps again. I opened the door to no one there, so I walked to the top of the steps and looked around in the rooms to find no one else around."

And sometimes things happen to our customers that are simply unexplainable:

"Jeff was working an evening by himself when he and a couple of customers heard walking near the door, then a few knocks on the door between the green room and the office. He thought someone had somehow gotten in through the back door. When he opened the door no one was there. He came back out to tell the customers no one was there, and they were all just standing there floored because they all heard it."

Sue and another employee, had been cleaning around the desk area with a bright yellow cleaning cloth. Sue's co-worker had just folded the cloth and placed it on a shelf under the desk. Within seconds, Sue saw a flash out of the corner of her eye and discovered that the cleaning cloth was now draped over her shoulder. Her co-worker had a horrified look on her face. Needing to lighten things up, as much for herself as her co-worker, Sue said, "It must be Mrs. Kitzmiller telling us we're not done cleaning yet."

One night, Sue was working with Don in the front office, during a time period when renovations were going on in the Green Room. The workers were gone from the Green Room, but both heard whistling coming from that room.

Then there was the family of four Sue and Don saw through the front window walking up to enter the office. The littlest boy was following everyone else in. When they all got into the office there was no little boy at the tail end of the procession. Sue asked the family if they'd forgotten the little boy outside. The family replied, "What little boy?" There were just three in the family.

Another time, Jeff Ritzman, the man who photographed the child ghost in the building, was photographing the interior for the internet using a 360-degree camera, which produced a striking panoramic view of the interior. When he finished, he asked if he might go back upstairs and conduct a "mini-investigation" on his own.

After several minutes he came back down stairs with a strange look on his face. It took a while to coax the story out of him, but he eventually told us that while he was investigating the upstairs bedroom, which then was being used occasionally by friends, he heard a male voice say, right in his ear, something about a pair of man's underwear that needed to be removed from beneath the bed.

The fact that the voice was so close to his ear and the oddness of the request shook up the seasoned paranormalist and he cut his investigation short and hurried downstairs.

Carol asked, "Well, did you check under the bed?" to which Jeff replied that he was too shaken to do so. Carol, being her curious and feisty self, immediately went upstairs. She had an amused look on her face as she came back down, a pair of men's black underwear in her hand.

A phone call to the people who last used the upstairs bedroom confirmed that, indeed, upon returning home the man had discovered that he'd inadvertently left a pair of his underwear behind.

One night Kayla, Eric, Carol and I were finishing up a day of work, sitting on the benches in the courtyard. It was after dark and relatively quiet in the courtyard, with a lull in the traffic out on Baltimore Street. There, in the area where Confederate soldiers, 160 years before, meandered around looking for food and water and dodging Yankee bullets from riflemen on Cemetery Hill, and where the Young women spirited a wounded Union soldier from under the rebels' noses, down the exterior stairs, we all heard footsteps quietly make their way down the stairs. The only problem: no living body was visible. "Did you hear that?" I asked. Everyone nodded and Kayla said, "That's not the first time we've heard it."

A couple lived for a while in the upstairs apartment in the Ghost House. She was sensitive to paranormal goings-on and had numerous experiences, besides the strange "feelings" that individuals who are tuned in to the Other World have.

Tangible evidence of the spirit presences in the house that she experienced were the sounds of footsteps on the interior stairs to the second floor, and across the first-floor rooms. It's probably fortunate that she was used to unexplained events in her life; these occurred on her first night in the house. She once saw a woman carrying something up the stairs.

She also recalled hearing what she called a basketball being bounced on the floor. Her partner—who is not sensitive to paranormal energies—also heard a ball bouncing on the stairs.

Other individuals have also heard footsteps on those stairs, including my co-author of *The Big Book of Pennsylvania Ghost Stories,* and *Cursed in Pennsylvania,* Patty Wilson.

The evidence for children's spirits still roaming the house was captured as well when midwestern psychic Rob Conover investigated the house. I video-taped his impressions while he toured the house, just to document the visit. Upon playback, in one segment of the tape there can be heard what sounds like a little girl singing in the background. No children were on the walk-through and everyone there was silent while Rob passed on his impressions.

Georgia soldiers' presence in the house has been documented via EVP—Electronic Voice Phenomena—the alleged voices of the dead recorded on electromagnetic tape or digital recorders. I've asked questions specific to the state of Georgia: "Have you ever been to Atlanta?" "Have you ever been to Savannah?" and so forth and have gotten positive responses; also, the garbled voice of a spirit we previously identified as a priest finishing a verse of the Lord's Prayer when we stopped reciting it; Mary Kitzmiller, when asked if she liked the cookies we set out per her repeated requests, answered, "I hate them"; a friend who is also a gifted medium hearing an EVP recording of her recently deceased brother telling his daughter who was present that he loved her, never having mentioned it when he was alive; and that same brother appearing as a shadow behind our friend in a photo taken in the back room when the previous photo showed nothing; and finally, my own grandfather, John Pasko, who died before I was born, showed up during a past life regression session performed on myself. Unfortunately, though I would have liked to, I couldn't see him, but the mediums described him just like his photos that I had grown up with. They said they saw him nod and heard him say he was proud of me.

So, perhaps, in 1997, I inadvertently purchased not just a building from which to run the original ghost tours of Gettysburg, but a private laboratory in which experiments into the supernatural realms can be performed, gaining, little by little, bits and pieces of information about the invisible, hidden world that also occupies this world we can see, a world to which we are all, eventually, inexorably destined.

SPANGLER'S MEADOW

As flies to wanton boys,
Are we to the Gods;
They kill us for their sport.

—William Shakespeare, *King Lear*

It was only a few years ago that, when asked what was the most paranormally active place on the battlefield, I would answer "Spangler's Spring" since I had been hearing numerous stories arising from the area. Like many active sites in Gettysburg, the frequency of stories soon slowed down. But findings from a long-lost set of files reminded me of how supernatural activity ebbs and flows around the grounds of the great battlefield as if the ghosts had some kind of weird communications network and determine, periodically, where they will gather next.

Paranormally, the Spangler's Spring area at Gettysburg is most notorious for the sightings of a misty, translucent figure, identified as a woman, wearing a non-descript white dress or gown, slowly floating through the fields around the spring. She has been known for as long as she's been seen, as The Woman in White.

I have documented sightings from so long ago no sources are given, but the sightings are always described in the same way, from merely a specter, to an exact, detailed description by two nurses—trained observers, like doctors and police—of a mist rising from a glowing orb of light at the base of a tree near Spangler's Spring, and materializing into a full apparition of a beautiful young woman.

After knowing of the famed apparition for decades, finally I was given a hint as to the identity of the Woman in

White and wrote about it in an earlier *Ghosts of Gettysburg* book. This is a summary:

> A man and his wife who lived in a house on the Baltimore Pike just a few hundred yards from Spangler's Spring approached me after saying that they thought the Woman in White, although long dead, "lived" in their house. After the battle, the house, like so many others, had become a hospital for the wounded. I arranged a paranormal investigation with one of the prominent mediums with whom I've worked. The house had a central stairway that led to the upstairs hallway. Both husband and wife had seen, from the bottom of the stairs, the wispy figure of a woman dressed in white, cross the hallway above them. Their children had seen her as well and gave the same description.

As per protocol, no one told our medium anything about the house or the sightings. After nearly an hour and several impressions of other ghostly beings in the house the woman of the house finally asked our medium, "Do you get an impression of a woman dressed in white here?" The medium answered immediately: "Yes. That's the nun."

It suddenly struck me that some of the first to come to Gettysburg after the carnage as volunteer nurses were the Sisters of Charity from the convent of St. Joseph in Emmitsburg, Maryland. As many as 40 nuns with their distinctive white-winged head-coverings came to tend to the wounded. Could a nun, her spirit eternally devoted to the sick and desperately wounded, still be seeking those who needed her help? The owners of the house said that their woman in white wasn't a constant presence; I opined that was because she was splitting her time between the hospital here and looking for more wounded among the ghostly dead at Spangler's Spring, a few hundred yards away.

Apparently, there are other entities at Spangler's Spring as well. In another book I wrote about a fellow paranormal investigator who saw different forms of paranormal entities at the Spring: small, dark figures scurrying about the ground and trees near the Spring—not so much human, but perhaps elementals, who are said to accompany spirits, as well as living humans, on supernatural missions.

Historically speaking, while Spangler's Spring is a famous landmark on the battlefield, Spangler's Meadow is not. Spangler's Spring is well-known, or at least remembered, partially because of a myth; Spangler's Meadow should be known for its history of blood shed there by exceedingly brave young men.

Spangler's Meadow

Early guides used to tell the tale of how men from both north and south fraternized like rival athletes after a game around the cool refreshing waters of Spangler's Spring after a warm day of a contest.

Getting water there, probably yes. Fraternizing, no. It was a fictional story of the tragic irony of countrymen fighting countrymen in a bitter civil war, shown in an emotional fable.

The combat was too ferocious near Abraham Spangler's spring for sitting around socializing with the enemy like it was a summer picnic at a family reunion. That fact is testified to by descriptions of the fighting at Spangler's Meadow, within sight of the spring.

Mr. Spangler's once-bucolic meadow to the east of his spring had been contested ground since daybreak, July 2. Confederates, ensconced among the trees, boulders and rock walls on the side of Culp's Hill facing the meadow had been picking off Union infantrymen since first light. One Federal soldier from the 2nd Massachusetts who was shot and unable to crawl back to his own lines, caught the merciful eye of one of his officers, Capt. Thomas R. Robeson, who took it upon himself to enter the kill-zone, pick the man up in his arms, and carry him, bullets kicking up the dust around him, back to the relative safety of their position.

The 2nd Massachusetts Infantry was assembled in a wooded area across Spangler's Meadow south of Spangler's Spring. After enduring the dangerous enemy fire for hours, around 10:00 A.M. they got the order to attack Confederates on the southern slope of Culp's Hill near the spring. Commanding the 2nd was Lt. Col. Charles R. Mudge, 24 years old, a graduate of Harvard and survivor of the hell of the Bloody Cornfield at Antietam the previous September.

Peering from the woods, he could see that they would have to cross 100 yards of open fields before striking the Confederate lines bristling with muskets and protected behind stone walls, jagged boulders and a rock ledge.

To his staff he said with eerie prescience that it was "murder but it was the order."

Midwesterners of the 27th Indiana would join the New Englanders for the assault with the two regiments totaling about 650 men.

Under cover of the trees and rocks of the rugged south slope of Culp's Hill were over 1,000 Confederates of Steuart's Brigade and the Virginians of Smith's Brigade.

The Bay Staters began the assault angling toward Mr. Spangler's Spring. They felt the sting of only skirmisher's fire at first until they neared the rising, craggy ground of Culp's Hill. Halting, they let loose a volley attempting to drive away the enemy riflemen, then resumed the advance. A few more steps and the ragged stone wall and strewn boulders exploded with a volley of rifle fire. In the memory of one of the assaulting troops their right flank seemed to simply melt away.

For centuries, before the advent of radio communications on the battlefield, the term "Rally 'round the flag" was more than just a patriotic saying. If you wanted a symbol of the heart and soul of a military unit, it was "the colors" fluttering high above, when at ground level everything was wrapped in the heavy layer of smoke produced by black powder. Spotting the flags often meant the difference between life and death or having the regiment retreat without you, being captured and sent to starvation and other unimaginable horrors of a military prison.

So members of the color guard were chosen for their physical bravery as well as their physical height: they had to possess both. But being brave and tall on a battlefield is not always a good thing. Often, the color guard paid for their gallantry, steadfastness and conspicuousness. On this particular July morning, the color guard of the 2nd Massachusetts paid dearly with the most valuable currency of all: their lives.

They had not completed the first fifty yards of the advance before the color-sergeant doubled-over with a mortal wound. Next to be shot dead was the color-corporal who grabbed the flag. Down went another corporal, shot picking up the flag.

Private Stephan A. Cody grabbed the colors, stood on a rock to rally his comrades, defiantly waving the flag in the rebels' faces—until they killed him, too. The fifth man to seize the flag somehow, inexplicably, made it through the storm of lead that scythed down the others.

But great-hearted, compassionate Captain Robeson, who had earlier saved the life of one of his soldiers by carrying the wounded man back to his lines under fire, did not survive the fusillade; nor did the young Harvard alum Colonel Mudge. He had escaped his fate in the maelstrom of farmer Miller's Cornfield at Antietam only to be shot in the neck not far from farmer Spangler's Spring near Gettysburg. Both died later of their wounds.

The 27th Indiana, following the 2nd Massachusetts, angled their attack more across Mr. Spangler's meadow and the rifle fire coming from the rock wall on the other side of it. Just a few steps out of the woods and into the meadow, and Confederate fire pummeled them. Partway across, the men soon found themselves in more trouble, in addition to the fire of the concealed Confederates.

They discovered that the open field was wet, swampy ground that sucked at their shoes and bogged them down. They were denied a quick rush across the open field. With no cover, their advance reduced to a crawl as the southerners fired another volley from the rocky slope. Maj. Thomas F. Colgrove, who was, as an officer, mounted, had an excellent but dangerous view of the ongoing battle. He was shocked to see his right three companies seemingly shot down all at once. Historian and former Superintendent at Gettysburg National Military Park, Harry W. Pfanz wrote in his excellent and comprehensive book, *Gettysburg: Culp's Hill and Cemetery Hill,* that other witnesses said that it looked like "the earth had opened and swallowed the regiment."

Like the astute veterans they were, the men of the 27th Indiana would wait for the rebels to fire a volley and begin to re-load; it was then they would advance a few steps, fire, then halt to re-load their own rifle muskets. But the tactical advantage remained with the southerners on defense, concealed behind the rock walls and boulders, while the Midwesterners stood in battle lines in an open field.

Once again, the Confederates picked the most conspicuous targets: the color guard of the 27th.

The original color sergeant of the 27th went down. So did, one-by-one, with agonizing precision, the next six men to pick up the flag. There is a small block monument in the middle of Spangler's Meadow recalling the men of the color guard's rock-solid courage and unwavering dedication to duty. Slowly, almost reluctantly, the men of the 27th Indiana withdrew from the once peaceful meadow, leaving it spattered with their own blood.

Sadly, the soldiers from Massachusetts were not yet through their ordeal. For another ten minutes they went head-to-head with the concealed Confederates. Colonel Mudge's replacement later wrote; the fighting was "at the shortest range I have ever seen two lines engaged...."

Finally, torn by enemy musket balls, they retreated from the killing ground, abandoning their original position to the relative shelter of a stone wall on the south side of the meadow.

Though the Confederates launched a counter-attack across the deadly, body-strewn meadow, they too found it nothing but a field of slaughter and retired to the safety of their woods and rock walls of Culp's Hill. Spangler's Meadow was left to the dead and dying.

The 2nd Massachusetts lost 22 killed in action or mortally wounded and 112 wounded. Those figures account for over forty percent of their original strength, a huge loss for such a short fight.

The 27th Indiana lost 18 killed or mortally wounded and 93 wounded, about thirty percent of the men who began the assault.

Their conspicuous gallantry did not go unnoticed. Word of their stubborn, bloody and resolute fighting quickly made its way up the chain of command to their leaders. Deemed pretty much used up after their battle in Spangler's Meadow, the 27th Indiana and 2nd Massachusetts were being withdrawn. As the tattered and bloody remnants of the 2nd marched past the headquarters of General Slocum, their Corps commander, Slocum and his staff were standing outside. Someone recognized the regiment and pointed them out. As the staff watched them pass, Slocum removed his hat, followed by the rest of the staff, as soldier to soldier, they honored the regiment in awed silence.

From my archives of the "Lost Files," I have gleaned several more stories about the Spangler's Spring and Meadow area.

One August, a number of years back, a family was touring the battlefield on one of the commercial double-decker tour buses. Listening on headphones to the narration of the battle in that area, they rounded the bend to view Spangler's Meadow, and got a view of the Indiana Monument. Standing before it at attention and giving a soldier's salute was a man dressed in a blue uniform and complete kit of a Union soldier. As the bus drove by, he turned slightly toward the conveyance and lifted a hand in recognition, then moved closer to the monument as if to inspect it. The writer said she looked away and thought nothing of it, but upon looking back seconds later, couldn't see the man anymore. Anyone familiar with the area around the Indiana Monument knows that it is an open field with nowhere to hide. She shrugged it off and continued to listen to the recorded narration of the battle.

The woman thought no more about it until they were checking out of the James Gettys Hotel two days later when she casually began to tell the hotel clerk about the sighting of the Union soldier two days prior. Suddenly every member of her family stirred. It so happened that every one of the eight members had seen the same soldier and noticed that he had seemingly disappeared not to be seen again by any of them. Caught up in the tour narration, they had forgotten about the strange event until just then, and were amazed that they had all witnessed the same apparition.

Over the years, paranormalists have classified the various types of encounters with supernatural beings—ghosts, if you will. There are poltergeists—noisy ghosts that throw things around, flash lights and make noises. Most often experienced, especially at Gettysburg, are auditory apparitions, where the percipient hears voices, floors or doors creaking, and, most frequently, footsteps. Auditory apparitions make up approximately sixty percent of all the stories I have collected. Then there are the extremely rare "visuals": sightings of full-figure apparitions. These make up about ten percent of my collection.

Rarest of all would be where the visual apparition actually speaks to the percipient, a phenomenon known as an interactive or intelligent haunting.

A woman wrote to the National Park Service at Gettysburg to ask about a strange encounter she, her husband and two others had while touring through the Spangler's Spring area.

It was dusk, on an October evening, when they drove through. They spotted a young man dressed as a soldier sitting with his back against one of the large boulders before a small campfire, apparently mending a sock he had worn a hole through. His musket and haversack were leaning against the boulder. His uniform was worn and tattered. The tourists knew that Spangler's Spring was not an "official" National Park Service campground and that fires were strictly prohibited. (It wasn't until later years that the Park Service began allowing approved reenactor groups to stay at Spangler's Spring overnight in return for putting on soldier demonstrations during the day.)

When a Park Ranger drove through the area within sight of the young man and his fire and did not stop, the group assumed the "soldier" must have permission to be there that evening. Certainly, the Ranger would have stopped to chase the young man off. They stopped and parked in a nearby lot and approached the "soldier."

They all spoke with him briefly. They asked questions, which he answered, as the writer put it, "in a vague 'Civil War' manner." He pointed to the woods and told them he was waiting for his friends and, cryptically, that "they would probably see some action later."

The woman wrote that they are frequent Gettysburg visitors, as well as Civil War enthusiasts, being members of the venerable North-South Skirmish Association and were very familiar with the uniform and accoutrements of the young soldier. Perhaps referring to the fact that he never "broke character" continuing to answer in a "vague Civil War manner," they even were willing to concede that he certainly was a "well-versed Civil War period reenactor."

Except that later, when they mentioned the event to Park Officials, they were told in no uncertain terms that "NO ONE" is allowed there, especially with a campfire, which made the patrolling Park Ranger's non-action even more confusing. In their letter to me she asked if I could verify if someone was given permission over the days they visited to camp and have a campfire.

Unfortunately, at the time I received the letter, most of my colleagues from my career in the National Park Service had moved on; there was really no one I could ask about it. But she did enclose a letter she received after she wrote the Park to ask about her group's encounter. The Ranger politely informed her that she was correct that no reenactors are allowed to camp with fires on the battlefield, but occasionally there are some Civil War enthusiasts who do break the rules. Perhaps this was the explanation for their encounter?

It does explain their experience...at least in our rational, temporal, worldly terms. It does not explain, however, how a Park Ranger on patrol, whose job it was to notice something out of the ordinary—like an intruder with a campfire violating federal law—would miss something plainly visible to a group of tourists.

A paranormal theory known as a "warp," or rip in the fabric of time, opening a temporary gap in our reality to show us an earlier reality, might explain it.

Two stories from people who had contributed to my previous *Ghosts of Gettysburg* books ended up in the "Lost Files." They also occurred in the Spangler Meadow area.

One woman was walking along East Confederate Avenue, the battlefield road around Culp's Hill that ends in Spangler's Spring. It was a late October afternoon. She had just said hello to a woman who had crossed Spangler's Meadow and entered the road going the other way. She casually looked up the hill to her right and saw the figure of a man in full uniform appearing in a blue haze. Because of his outfit she recognized him as a Union soldier, in his early 20s, who appeared to be nervously looking around, first toward the side of the hill, then toward the cluster of rocks. She looked away for a moment and when she looked back, he had vanished.

Reaching the parking lot for Spangler's Spring she saw what she thought to be the reason for his apprehension. Exiting a car was a woman, a Union reenactor and two Confederate reenactors moving toward where she had seen him. The question remains: was he reacting to people or events in the real world? Could he see our world just as we can sometimes see into his?

Another woman wrote about an experience she and three members of her family had one mid-August night near Spangler's Meadow.

Although the Park was officially closed for the evening, they ventured onto the hallowed ground. It is hard to believe with the frenetic daytime tourist visitation, but the battlefield at night can be a relaxing place. Having lived in three historic houses on the battlefield during my career as a Park Ranger, I felt the "mood swings" the battlefield seems to have. There were times on night patrol when the weather was perfect, and a calm could be felt on the field—or at least the part of the field I was occupying at the time. I often wonder if I noticed it because much of the rest of the time the battlefield exuded a kind of spiritual turmoil, barely felt, like a subliminal vibration or frequency that sometimes subsided. I would pull over in the official vehicle, grab the hand-held radio, and take a short night-time walk through Devil's Den or atop Little Round Top just to stretch my legs. Of course, there were other times when I would get ready to exit the vehicle and a chill would hit and something would say to me, *no... maybe next time.* No explanation. Just a *feeling.*

As they drove the darkened road, her son's girlfriend exclaimed that she had just seen a group of people behind them. At first the driver thought it might have been a bunch of kids partying and turned to the right, inadvertently going the wrong way on East Confederate Avenue, to see them. As she made the turn, the entire family was shocked to see a Confederate soldier in a tattered gray uniform leaning against a tree. To their horror, they looked into the little gully off to the side of the road and saw the twisted form of another soldier, pasty-white face contorted in agony. But the worst was yet to come.

In front of him, tossed as if by some violent malevolence, were the bodies of a dozen or so soldiers, as if they had been massacred with bodies sprawled upon on another, and body parts spread out for twenty yards. There was no movement. They were as still as death could make them. What really got to the family was that when their high beams hit them, not one blinked, flinched or moved to cover their eyes from the sudden bright light piercing the dark. In fact, she described their eyes as deep set, dark circles, looking as if great pain had been inflicted not only upon their earthly forms, but upon their very souls before they left those forms.

The shock of what they saw was so great that some of the family started screaming. They vacated the area as quickly as possible and when they left the battlefield, they ended up talking about the experience nearly until dawn.

They returned the next day. Exiting the vehicle, they walked where the bodies had been sprawled. The terrain was the same, but she wrote that the trees seemed larger. Someone noticed that there was no evidence that humans had been in the area: no cigarette butts, no gum wrappers, no footprints, not even the smallest saplings were bent or broken.

And finally, from the "Lost Files" comes a story from visitors who periodically camped in the commercial campground that once occupied the corner of the Baltimore Pike and Colgrove Avenue, which leads to Spangler's Spring and the adjacent meadow.

Their favorite site was in the back of the campground, nearest the stone wall that separated the campground and the National Park boundary. One of the campers' favorite pastimes was to sit on the monument to the 2nd Massachusetts Regiment and read until dusk.

One night they were sitting around the campfire when their friend's daughter saw something just outside the fire's glow. She described it as someone in a white outfit passing just along their visual perimeter. But there was something strange about it: it "didn't look real," she said. "They were almost floating." Her mother had caught it out of the corner of her eye, but her daughter had gotten a better look. They talked and confirmed that there was no living being in the area.

The writer admitted that she was actually relieved. "Ghosts, finally!" she caught herself thinking.

The next morning, they casually mentioned their experience to the owners of the campground who didn't seem surprised at all. To try to explain what they may have seen, the owners proceeded to tell them the story—at least one of the numerous stories—of Spangler Spring's most frequent and notorious ghost. The letter did not say whether the observers were satisfied or horrified by the fact that they too may have seen the famous, yet elusive, Woman in White.

This winter of the next day, leaving the pink brush speckled
[illegible faded text]

HORRORS BEYOND HORRORS

"...mystics have claimed over the millennia, we are not simply bodies of dense matter, but also intrinsically refined spirit, which constantly strives to connect with its own world."

—Lynn Picknett, *Mary Magdalene*

"What we have called matter is energy, whose vibration has been so lowered as to be perceptible to the senses. Matter is spirit reduced to the point of visibility. There is no matter."

—Albert Einstein

When we talk about ghosts, what we're really talking about is energy. *Everything* is energy. Energy has different frequencies, some vibrating slowly, some rapidly, and some at just the right frequency for humans to see or hear.

Along the vast spectrum of electromagnetic energy, there is just a tiny sliver of wavelengths and associated frequencies that the human eye can perceive. Anything of the vast reality beyond that is invisible and needs special augmentative equipment for us to even know about it.

Hearing is more complicated, depending upon distance from the source, the medium through which the sound is propagated, the type of sound (music, speech, infra-sounds), the tone and so forth. Once again, in the vast frequency range of sound, humans can only hear between 20 and 20,000 hertz.

If something exists on either side of those frequencies, to humans it doesn't exist.

So ghosts, who appear to us to move in and out of existence may only be changing their frequency to enter and leave the world we perceive.

But also, for them to exist in our world, there is another factor that must be present:

Us.

Someone be there to be lucky (or unlucky) enough to perceive the ghost.

So, the amount of activity at special places like Gettysburg also has to do with the number people visiting the site.

In other words, while the ghosts may be active, you need a living person to witness them and report their experiences.

Little Round Top had been undergoing a much-needed re-vitalization and had been closed to the public. Very often, in the supernatural realm, when the physical *status quo* of a building or site is altered, there appears to be an increase in paranormal activity. Since there is only a construction crew to witness anything that happens (as opposed to the thousands of tourists who visit the site every day in the summer) there are virtually no reports coming from the area.

But imagine: You are the spirit remnants of Brigadier General Stephen H. Weed, shot on the crest of Little Round Top and paralyzed from the neck down, or Artillerist Lieutenant Charles Hazlett, who, leaning over to get Weed's last commands, was shot through the head, falling across Weed's numb body; or Colonel Paddy O'Rorke, commanding the 140th New York, shot through the neck halfway down the hill, or Colonel Strong Vincent, brigade commander, rallying the 44th New York Regiment, shot down in that mêlée. Now, there are living humans with digging equipment scratching and scraping into the earth around the very spot upon which you fell after being shot—the earth that soaked up your own life's blood. Would whatever remained of your personality, from wherever it transmigrated to, at least be a little interested in what they were doing to a place so sacred, if only to you alone?

When asked about the most haunted sites of Gettysburg, however, I will mention two places which seem to consistently produced strange, otherworldly sightings and out-of-place-and-time events: Devil's Den and the adjacent Triangular Field.

Devil's Den

The mere name "Devil's Den" conjures up a place of hell-like horrors and harrowing death. Seeing the place, especially for the first time, and trying to imaging men engaged in mortal combat around and atop the towering boulders and then falling, collapsing helplessly wounded into the twisted narrow crevices, sends a chill up one's spine. If the men who fought there lived long enough to learn the locals' name for the jumble of granite rocks and building-sized boulders, they would no doubt concur that the name, especially under combat conditions, was appropriate.

As well, anyone who has visited Devil's Den in late afternoon of an early July day—about the time the battle occurred—will quickly realize, the huge boulders heat up, like an immense old-fashioned bake-oven, and radiate their heat, as well as block any cooling breeze, ripping the sweat from human bodies until you practically become insensible, so that the Devil's Den can easily be called the Devil's Oven.

Stories from the area weave their way through even the pre-battle history of the site. Appearing (as only ghosts can) from out of the pre-history of the earliest native populations and intruding into a more modern (if the late 18th Century can now be called that) setting, we have our very first Devil's Den ghost story, one of the first told of Gettysburg of a Native American—at the time an extinct culture to the area—emerging from a rip in reality to lead some lost desperate hunters from the jumble of rocks to safety.

Another famous story—and the first one I personally heard—from the mid-20th century, is of the young woman, visiting the top of the rocks alone, who is spoken to by a raggedly-dressed man, who then, inexplicably, disappears before her eyes. When she reports him to the Park Rangers and describes him, they are amazed at the accuracy with which she paints an image of a threadbare Texas soldier of the Confederate Army, whose fellow Lone-Star-Staters are given much of the credit for wresting the forlorn pile of rocks from the Yankees. Since the events he participated in occurred some 110 years before, he could have only, plausibly, been dead when she saw him.

Remarkably, he was documented as being seen at least twice more since then, as recounted in the chapter titled "Déjà vu," in *Ghosts of Gettysburg VIII*.

Gleaning the "Lost Files," I found a letter I received a few years back from a man who was visiting Devil's Den with his wife during the off-season in Gettysburg. It was a rare opportunity, as he recognized, to be without the hordes of visitors the location attracts. He was pleased to have the place, "all to themselves." It may have been the off-season, but, as they were soon to realize, they were far from alone.

It was shortly after sunset as they explored the Den. They were walking along the road, passing a particular large, flat-topped rock, when his wife suddenly stopped. She said she had just heard a drum beat. Then she said she heard what sounded like explosions coming from behind her, on Little Round Top.

Just as she said it her husband looked to his left and was startled to see a short, crouching figure on the flat rock, staring right at him. Shocked at the closeness of the individual, he jumped back, only to see the figure stand and run along the rock away from him. He remembered that the image wore a small cap reminding him of the soldiers' kepis so common during the Civil War. Regaining his composure—but only momentarily—he watched as the human figure reached the edge of the rock, then, inexplicably, de-materialized.

On another off-season trip to Gettysburg, this time alone, the man was again near Devil's Den, his parked car, the only one in the lot. He began to ascend Warren Avenue which runs between Little Round Top and Big Round Top. Along the road, on the right-hand side was a dirt pathway that once led to the stone restroom building, where he stopped momentarily. He saw, about 80 feet down the path, what he thought was a small campfire… "yet," he wrote, "it didn't look right." He observed that the fire was not flickering, but also determined it was not a modern light like a flashlight.

Curious, he began to walk down the pathway, to see if it really was a fire. As he approached, slowly, the light began to fade. A few more steps, and the "fire" died down even more, not as if someone was putting it out, but as if it was on some kind of a dimmer switch, slowly dying down. Suddenly he got an uncomfortable feeling like something he could feel but not see was advising him to leave. By that time, the discomfort he felt had grown perceptibly and, convinced that what he saw was not a real fire, he turned and left.

Phantom fires are no new thing to Gettysburg. There are the persistent rumors, on the anniversary of the nights before the battle, of flickering spots of light all along the dark, forbidding, eastern face of the distant South Mountain Range, reminiscent of the hundreds of camps—some signifying their last night on earth—of Confederates, defying time and reality, once again participating in the Great Invasion of Pennsylvania. Even Park Rangers have seen them on the darkened battlefield, but when they visit the site where the fires burned, they find no smoldering embers, no hot coals or smoke, nothing to testify to anything but illusionary fires from a time long gone by.

But the story of the vision of the soldier brought to mind another story sent to me. Perhaps this story actually belongs in one of my "Déjà vu" chapters, since it resembles the first so vividly—except for one horrifying detail.

It was, appropriately, July 2, the anniversary of the unimaginable carnage that took place on that very ground. A woman and her brother were visiting the battlefield. Though it was early in the day, Devil's Den still had its share of visitors. Looking at a line of trees near the Den, she was struck by the appearance of what she thought was a Confederate reenactor. He was sitting with his legs drawn up to his chest with his head resting upon his knees. She described his uniform as "really tattered and torn," and that he seemed to be very weary (this in spite of the fact that it was early in the day.) She asked her brother if he could make out what reenactment regiment he was in, so that she might compliment him to his commanding officer. Her brother asked where the soldier was. She pointed him out to her brother, but he said he saw no one. She looked back to watch the soldier, wondering if maybe her brother needed a stronger prescription for his glasses.

She wrote that for some reason, she couldn't seem to taker her eyes off the weary, ragged soldier. For a long time she stared, until he raised his head and turned to look at her. It was then she made a disturbing observation: "What should have been his face was just a skull."

However, repulsed she may have been at seeing the shocking sight, it was mitigated by the horrifying impression that he was trying to communicate with her, and the fact that she couldn't understand what he wanted to convey. She thought she heard her brother say, "Tell them", and turned to him to ask him what he meant. But the words did not come from her sibling.

She looked back at the soldier only she could see and heard, louder and with more urgency, "Tell them! Tell them!" Confused about what the soldier wanted she asked out loud, "Tell them what?"

She felt a hard poke to her ribs and heard her brother telling her that she was making a scene in front of the other visitors, then asking if she was okay. He still insisted that he saw and heard nothing out of the ordinary; she vowed to get him an eye and ear exam as soon as they were home.

One theory that attempts to explain paranormal events is the Alternate Realities Theory, that more than one reality timeline can coexist alongside another. Usually only one reality is observable or experienced by all of us at one time; sometimes, apparently, more than one reality can be experienced at the same time. Some theories in Quantum Physics appear to back this up. The theory that entire other universes may coexist with ours has been advanced, as well as the theory that we may exist on these other timelines in other realities at the same time we exist on this one. One prominent physicist from Harvard has written about realities— worlds similar to ours—that may exist simultaneously on "branes," sheet-like membranes containing their own realities. What if these "branes" are flexible, like rubber sheets, and bend and bulge according to whatever physical law acts upon them at the moment? What if they are not only malleable but permeable as well, and the two realities occasionally cross-over, entering the other? What if some of them lag in time behind our current reality, say, 160 or so years? Could this be where our temporary visions of the past come from?

Courage in combat comes in many forms. There are some men who just have no need for fear and go about their dangerous duties as if there was no danger at all. Others, like

Thomas J. "Stonewall" Jackson and Robert E. Lee, professed such faith in a higher being who orchestrates one's life, that worrying about danger—not to mention attempting to dodge it—is useless. Others have a stronger sense of duty that overcomes fear.

Gettysburg veteran Brigadier General Joshua Chamberlain of Maine seemed to agree that there are different kinds of courage displayed on the battlefield. In his classic book, The Passing of the Armies, he wrote revealingly about fear infecting men in battle: "A soldier has something else to think about. Most men at the first, or at some tragic moment, are aware of the present peril, and perhaps flinch a little by an instinct of nature and sometimes accept the foregoing confession, —as when I have seen men pin their names to their breasts that they may not be buried unknown. But any action following the motive of fear is rare, —for sometimes I have seen men rushing to the front in a terrific fire, 'to have it over with.'

"But, as a rule, men stand up from one motive or another— simple manhood, force of discipline, pride, love, or bond of companionship— 'Here is Bill; I will go or stay where he does.'"

Chamberlain referenced an officer—like himself—as being "so absorbed by the sense of responsibility for his men, for his cause, or for the fight, that the thought of personal peril has no place whatever in governing his actions. The instinct to seek safety is overcome by the instinct of honor."

Revealing a concept that might sound archaic or outdated, he continued: "There are exceptions. This is the rule and law of manhood: fearlessness in the face of all lesser issues because he has faced the greater—the commanding one."

All soldiers, of course, must embody some kind of courage to simply persevere. You must believe you have some sort of fighting chance of living just to enter the zone of conflict. Civil War Color-bearers, however, embodied courage of the highest kind, because they were targets—and they knew it.

As I have written before, the colors—the flags of the regiment—were the focal point, amidst the smoke and confusion and insanity of a Civil War battle, of every man in the unit. The regiment went where the colors went: seen above the haze of black powder smoke, if they moved forward, so moved the regiment toward the enemy; rearward, and the unit withdrew.

Of course, the enemy knew about this tool for communication, and so made the colors a special focus of their fire, taking down the color guard, men chosen for their larger size, thus making them easy targets. Casualties in, and life expectancies of, the color guard were horrific.

In the fighting in and around Devil's Den where the smoke seemed to cling to the rocks, two flags betray the violence aimed at the men of the color guard. According to Harry W. Pfanz in Gettysburg: The Second Day, the flag of the 4th Maine bore thirty-two bullet holes and two made by flying artillery shell fragments. Their opponents in the fighting, the 20th Georgia's flag had taken thirty-eight minié balls and forty-nine perforations by shell fragments, many from Smith's Battery atop Devil's Den.

Once again, a letter seemingly risen from the dead of the "Lost Files," came to light. A man and his nephew were visiting Gettysburg on Labor Day weekend. They'd gotten up early Saturday morning to beat the crowds onto the battlefield, which they did. They started their tour around 6:00 A.M. and reached Devil's Den about 8:00. Devil's Den was deserted, no cars, no people. They walked to the top of the jumble of boulders, passing the sniper's position, made famous by the photographer's staging of the body of a young, dead Confederate, and started back down the walking path toward the parking lot. As they descended, they were surprised to see a man dressed in a Confederate uniform walking along the road that winds through the Den, about 50 yards away.

They stopped to watch him pass. The writer saw his soft felt hat, trousers just short enough for a glimpse of his ankle high brogans, short jacket common to southern infantrymen, a belt and wooden canteen. The outfit was "worn but not shabby." He guessed his age to be around 25 to 30, his height to be around 5' 10", with a lean frame and dark hair curled around his coat collar.

He was walking past them from left to right, into the Den. Though he was in view for a minute or so, they never saw his face because his head was turned looking toward Little Round Top, which they saw still had no visitors on it.

One other thing they noticed was that he carried a flag rolled up on its staff in his hand. The writer remarked to his nephew that he thought it was a Texas "Lone Star" flag. He passed briefly from their view behind the boulders near them, but in the few seconds it took for them to continue down to the roadway, he had disappeared from sight. They were surprised. "At the pace he was walking and the distance he had to travel to get around the bend he should have still been in sight. The only other way was to scale the south face of the boulders which I believe are about 20 feet high."

They got into their car and drove around the bend following the curving road to the top of Devil's Den, heading toward the once blood-soaked Wheatfield. Just before they entered the woods, the writer glanced back at Devil's Den. "There he was, standing on the top of the highest boulder facing Little Round Top and waving a Texas flag back and forth. Little Round Top was still unoccupied."

They watched him for about 20 seconds before continuing through the Wheatfield. They decided to go back through Devil's Den to try and find the soldier. Because of the one-way roads, it took them about 15 minutes to return to the site. By then there were tourists, but no soldier. They hadn't seen him walk out as they drove back to Devil's Den and wouldn't see him walking as they followed the one-way road again through the Wheatfield.

And if Devil's Den hasn't satisfied the curious seekers of remnant spirits left on the battlefield by their once living comrades, the unusually-shaped Triangular Field has its own secrets to reveal.

Triangular Field

Continuing along the same Crawford Avenue that leads you into the jumble of boulders, a visitor can drive around ascending curves to the top of Devil's Den. Once through, on the other side of Devil's Den on the left is a field once encompassed by a three-sided stone wall. Sloped so as it was impossible to plow, it was used for grazing animals. It contains a number of depressions that appear to be abandoned gravesites, but are merely evidence that the field of death was once quarried for granite; the depressions were not there during the battle.

Over the millennia, human combat has had a long struggle to become more organized. Mobs of anywhere from a few men to thousands crashing together attempting to hack each other down, warfighting has gradually developed through the ages, from virtual chaos to detailed, highly planned affairs. But, even the most well-trained, meticulous military planners will admit that rarely do plans survive past the first contact of armies. Heavyweight boxing champion Mike Tyson probably said it best: "Everyone has a plan until they get punched in the face."

Napoleonic tactics were taught at the United States Military Academy at West Point and other military schools (such as The Virginia Military Institute) to the future commanding officers who would fight the American Civil War. They involved linear tactics—lines of soldiers maneuvering like so many wooden blocks to envelop or attack an enemy's flank or rear—which worked well on the open battlefields of the European theater where Napoleon fought so successfully.

But attempting to maneuver like blocks in lines in the tangled, wooded, hilly, rocky terrain of American battlefields was something different altogether. The lines they practiced keeping straight on drill fields would get hung up, bend, and fall apart over rough terrain, producing stragglers. Men in the rear lines would get shot, stumble and fall into the forward lines causing confusion. Men in the front lines would go down, tripping up those behind as they tried to advance. And all of this going on while attempting to leap rocks, stone walls, and fallen timber, untangling from briars, climbing or descending hills and dodging trees.

Again, from my "Lost Files," I retrieved an account from a woman whose family had read my accounts of cameras failing inexplicably in the Triangular Field and wanted to test the ghosts there. Fortunately, (but perhaps disappointingly) all their photos turned out just fine. But the ghosts of the Triangular Field had another way of making their presence known.

As they made their way down the slope, the woman's daughter complained loudly, "Mommy, somebody pushed me!" Without turning around, the woman told her husband to stop joking around and to leave their daughter alone. Again, the child cried out that someone had pushed her.

She turned around, expecting to see her husband laughing at his pranking their little girl. Instead, she saw her husband's face "white as a sheet. Even his lips were white!" She said she had never seen such terror on his face before or since, and he started babbling, "Come on!" he said. "Let's go! Come on! It's time to leave!"

Returning to their car, her husband swore that he had not touched their daughter, who said that it felt like two hands were on her back pushing her forward. Then she added, "Somebody didn't want me to be there. They wanted me to leave." The woman wrote, at that point, hearing her daughter's understanding of the reason why she was pushed, chills ran up and down her entire body.

The man who had encountered the crouching figure in Devil's Den from an earlier story was visiting the Triangular Field the next night. He walked to the stone wall that ran along the road and watched some "ghost hunters" down in the field snapping pictures. Deciding to follow his "gut" feeling that "something just wasn't quite right to my right and at the upper corner of the stone fence." He walked toward that corner of the field and sat on a large stone there.

(My circle of paranormalists calls this kind of investigating "intuition forward"—following even the smallest intuitive feeling on where to go to investigate. "Hands-on" equipment, such as dowsing rods and pendulums are used, then later, if necessary, backed up by more sophisticated electronic equipment. With this method, a new paranormal investigator doesn't need to lay out a great deal of money or even be an experienced medium to begin investigating.)

He sat for a while trying to figure out his feelings until the other ghost hunters approached. He asked if they had any success in the field and received a negative response. He told them that he had been feeling some "pretty odd things" in that corner and asked if they wanted to continue their investigation there. They started to snap photos, and to their astonishment began to get "swirling and spiraling lights coming out of the ground by the corner of the fence by the trees." He said the swirling lights were of various colors, and all unseen to the naked eye. The investigators ran some experiments to determine if the flashes on their cameras or other gear they were using were the causes of the strange lights, invisible to all but the cameras. They were satisfied that their equipment was not the source, and that all the activity was coming from that one spot. The man opined: "A vortex, perhaps?"

I am reminded of some of my earlier visits to the Triangular Field. During a visit around 1991 with renowned psychic Karyol Kirkpatrick, when I chronicled her first-ever visit to the Triangular Field in *Ghosts of Gettysburg II,* she pointed out the very corner of the field mentioned above. Sounding much like the indigenous peoples who once lived—and perhaps themselves fought and died—over the ground upon which we stood, she said that she felt the very trees that remained from the battle were weeping because there was more sorrow than they could absorb.

Other visitors I brought to the Triangular Field come to mind. In *Ghosts of Gettysburg IV,* I recounted the story of the late Cecil Downing, a Pennsylvania master dowser who had discovered over 800 successful wells in his lifetime, who had dowsed other places on the battlefield for the energy they contained and released. Cecil had also been drawn to that particular corner of the once hideous field, dowsed just outside the corner and found an area of strong residual energy between three trees growing there. Two people who accompanied us noticed how the trees all grew away and limbless from the area between them, where Cecil's dowsing rod pointed to the earth, as if somehow repulsed from whatever negative energy had been left there.

Another individual and her family were visiting the Triangular Field around 9:00 P.M. shortly after their arrival in Gettysburg. All they knew about the place was that cameras often failed there. They were at the top of the field near the stone wall and noticed "an odd-looking tree right beside it." She said looking at it gave her a "weird vibe," not scary, but like there was something invisible to the eye by the tree, and admitted that she had never gotten this feeling before: "I did not want to go near that tree…still don't!!" She took a few pictures and retired to her hotel.

They returned the next evening, about 7:30, walked all the way to the bottom of the field and got their cameras ready to begin photographing. A video camera she was using began to "act up" then it shut off completely. She tried to eject the tape but, for no reason, the tape had come out of the case to jam the camera. For a few minutes she attempted to free the tape without success. Her husband came over and said, as a joke, "Please let us get our tape out," thinking, apparently, that he was speaking to no one. Suddenly, the tape released. The woman pulled a fresh tape from her bag, inserted it and went to close the camera case. As if to show just who was in charge of the camera equipment in the field infamous for producing failed cameras, the door to the case would not close. She mentioned in her letter that after owning the camera for two years she never had a problem with closing it.

Climbing out of the Triangular field she mentioned to her husband her feelings about the tree in the corner of the field, which he teased her about. They reached the top of the field and suddenly heard a strange noise come from the lower left corner. Coyote was their first thought, but when it reverberated through the field three more times, they realized the sound was unidentifiable, but a sound stranger than any they had heard before.

After getting their still photos developed, they discovered the weird orbs, unseen when the photos were taken, believed by many paranormalists to be associated with ghostly activity.

The first few pictures she took of the tree that had disturbed her so much came out fine…except for one which shows a "big white bright substance taking up a good portion of the pic." But it had been a perfectly clear night. A photo from the second night shows what they believe to be a hazy but distinctly human figure peering at them from a distance.

Most ghost investigation equipment is designed around age-old beliefs about how ghosts manifest themselves in this dimension we—the living—occupy. It's pretty much agreed upon that a spirit will cause chills or a reduction in temperature *before* it is seen or heard (as opposed to *after* when a chill might be just a reaction to fear.) Therefore, a remote thermometer would be a good thing to scan a room with to detect spirits. (Outdoors, perhaps not so effective since the sensing beam spreads out after several feet.) Also, ghosts are known to "make the hair on the back of your neck stand up." This may be an indication of some kind of electromagnetic quality, perhaps static electricity, that can be attributed to ghosts. (This may also be why animals, because of all their fur, seem to make good "ghost detectors.)

High-end digital cameras are often in the ghost hunter's kit, as well as expensive digital voice recorders, so sensitive they will pick up the proverbial "pin drop." Those costly recorders may be perfect for bootlegging concerts, but EVP—the alleged voices of the dead—is, by definition, *Electronic* Voice Phenomena, and does not use vibrating air molecules to be embedded on a digital chip, but silent electromagnetic waves to do so.

You can literally spend thousands of dollars on electronic equipment designed specifically for "ghost hunting" when you may already have all you need at home.

Several years ago, a man who was investigating the Triangular Field for EVP had brought along a simple magnetic compass and placed it on one of the stone walls. He started his recorder and as he was taking a picture into the woods, he noticed that the compass needle slowly began to move away from north and point towards the high side of the Triangular Field in the direction of Devil's Den.

He asked a question: "Are you guys trying to tell me you want to get up that hill there?"

Like most EVP researchers, (not counting the ones who are mediums and can already hear spirits) he heard nothing. But when he returned home and played the recorder, he heard a drum roll recorded, not heard when he had asked the question.

He also wrote about his compass needle leaving the "north" position while investigating other parts of the battlefield, sometimes remaining for five minutes or longer "off-north."

During another investigation near Spangler's Spring he watched a "soccer ball-sized orb slowly glided down from Culp's Hill." It reached the small, rocky hill near the parking area for Spangler's Spring and vanished. He said it moved as smoothly as a leaf on a small stream. Behind it he could see a small "contrail" as it moved along. Some orb "debunkers" claim that orbs are merely dust too close to the camera lens that appear out of focus. Maybe some orbs in photographs, but certainly not ones seen with the naked eye.

I've written about Jeff Prechtel in previous *Ghosts of Gettysburg* volumes. It was Jeff, along with his artist father Don, whom I accompanied on a historical research mission through the Triangular Field that gave us more information on the paranormal aspects than historical of the land.

Don was doing a painting of the Confederate assaults up the hill, so we all spread out across the field to take photos. One by one, each of our expensive professional cameras stopped working. We gave up our mission, but as we were driving out of the area, the cameras all began working again.

On another trip to Gettysburg years later, Jeff was on his own exploring and photographing the strangely-shaped (and even more strangely-affected) field. After he returned home and inspected his photos, he noticed something strange at the bottom of the Triangular Field.

It looked like he had taken a photo of a line of troops, their light-colored faces visible against the dark background of the woods at the bottom of the field. There are at least ten faces that can be seen. As well, the original photograph is in color and dark jackets and sky-blue pants—the colors Union soldiers wore at the time of the Civil War—are clearly discernable from the darker background.

Granted, at the time of the fighting in the Triangular Field, that ground was eventually over-run by Confederates. But the question is: did Jeff somehow capture ghostly Union skirmishers out ahead of the Union line, or perhaps Union spirit-soldiers that roamed the area at the bottom of the hill *after* the fighting?

Did his camera accidentally pierce the flimsy veil that is the only thing that separates us from the dead, themselves?

Ghosts in Triangular Field
Photo by Jeff Prechtel

WHERE DREAMS CAME TO DIE

...You are not wrong, who deem
That my days have been a dream;
Yet if hope has flown away
In a night, or in a day,
In a vision, or in none,
Is it therefore the less gone?
All that we see or seem
Is but a dream within a dream.

—Edgar Allan Poe

Ask nearly any visitor to Gettysburg to show you the Bliss Farm on the Gettysburg Battlefield and you will likely be met with a confused gaze. Ask a local and your odds of receiving that same thoughtful expression of searching one's memory without results are about the same.

Ask a serious historian—a Park Ranger or Licensed Battlefield Guide—and they will tell you that they can't show you the Bliss Farm either. Not because they don't know where it is, but because it doesn't exist anymore.

They can show you the site of the farm: nearly smack in the middle of one of the most famous battlefields in history—the field of Pickett's Charge. They can show you a number of monuments to the various military units that fought over the house and barn, easily visible from the Union lines on Cemetery Ridge and more easily visible from their extended picket lines along Long Lane. Some may tell you of the effect of the farm and its structures on the tactical arrangement of the climactic Confederate assault of July 3, 1863. They may even cite the farm's probable effect on the outcome of the battle around it.

Bliss Farm Site

But the once prominent, possibly even history-changing, farm buildings of William and Adeline Bliss vanished during the battle as a result of their tactical importance, the doggedness of those who fought over them, the egos of their commanders, and fire.

The man who could tell you the most about the Bliss Farm and its importance to the battle action is, sadly, no longer with us. Elwood "Woody" Christ was about as dedicated an historian as you could find. Educated in history at Gettysburg College, he remained in Gettysburg working as a Licensed Battlefield Guide, as well as for the Borough of Gettysburg, doing research on the numerous historic structures remaining within the Borough, and nominating many structures to the National Register of Historic Places. He also volunteered at the Adams County Historical Society, served on the Board of Directors for the Gettysburg Battlefield Preservation Association, and most importantly for this story, wrote a book: *"Over a Wide, Hot,...Crimson*

Plain": The Struggle for the Bliss Farm at Gettysburg July 2nd and 3rd, 1863.

Students of the Battle of Gettysburg soon realize that just about every major aspect of the battle has been studied, written about and argued over in the years since the great conflagration of souls. Voluminous tomes now fill libraries analyzing and re-analyzing the fighting, rarely altering much of our knowledge of the battle. Personally, I am now drawn to smaller publications placing minor actions of the battle under the microscope, so to speak. Woody's book on the Bliss Farm is just that kind of work.

His research informs us that the Blisses had moved over the years from New England to a farm in northern Pennsylvania, thence to Chautauqua County, New York. After losing to grim death several of their children and suffering through one too many severe New York winters, in 1857, they purchased some 53 acres of farmstead just west of the road to Emmitsburg south of Gettysburg, Pennsylvania. The next year William Bliss added seven more acres to the farm that was to become, not only the culmination of his dreams, but within five years some of the most blood-soaked ground on earth.

The house was described years after the battle as a two-story frame building about fifty feet in length with two cellar entrances. Typical for the superstitions of the area, the front had two doors, one for the day-to-day use of the living, and the other, ominously, for those who died in the family, to be used only once.

In addition to the house, there stood a massive barn, seventy-five feet in length, thirty-three feet wide with a ten-foot-high stone and brick basement for stables. There was a ten-foot-wide overhang that faced east to expand the upper floor storage area and provide shelter from the elements. The west side of the barn was "banked" with an earthen ramp to drive wagons and equipment into the upper floor. Doors adorned the front and windows the ends, with high, narrow, vertical slits on the second floor for ventilation. The barn was about sixty yards from the house.

Both stood on a small, flat knoll with an orchard. The farmstead had a lovely view: to the southeast, their neighbors were the Codoris living right along the Emmitsburg Road in their solid brick house with its massive barn; to the west were the McMillans in their wooden house with the magnificent view of the South Mountains; to the northwest were the few buildings of the Lutheran Theological Seminary, with its distinctive cupola rising above; and to the southeast two rolling hills. From the Bliss farm flowed a small creek called Stevens Run, curling its way north, then eastward around the town of Gettysburg, to empty into Rock Creek.

But by the end of June 1863, increasing military incursions into the area told everyone in and around Gettysburg that what had been feared for so long was coming true: the war that had been convulsing the rest of the country was on its way. The afternoon of June 30 brought the jingling of horse equipment and the clank of sabers to the roads in the Gettysburg area. By early morning of July 1, the rattling volleys of carbines and muskets and the boom of artillery convinced the Bliss family to go with the McMillans to the Jacob Weikert Farm on the Taneytown Road, behind the two hills, to escape the battle.

Though that area at first seemed safe, the incredible vastness of the battle that was about to engulf the area could not have been anticipated. The very next afternoon, July 2, the hill just to the west of the Weikert Farm would become a major battle site; its name would be coined by the soldiers and newspapermen— "Little Round Top"—and the flood of casualties, including several high-ranking officers, would overflow into the nearest structures of Jacob Weikert's farm.

But around dawn on July 2, additional Union soldiers arriving from Maryland along the Taneytown Road were sent to the top of the ridge just to the west of the Taneytown Road—the ridge that extended southward from the hill with the local cemetery with the large, brick, arched gate. Once along the ridge, now named after the cemetery, the Union commanders sent out skirmishers into the fields to the west. Some 250 men of the 1st Delaware marched out and ran into musket fire from Confederates who had gotten to the Bliss buildings earlier. Outnumbered, the Confederates began a retreat through the Bliss family orchard back toward their lines forming on the ridge that led south from the Seminary.

The Delaware men passed the Bliss barn and spread out in skirmish lines leaving some officers behind using the barn as their command post. They remained in that position for only a short while.

Confederates wanted the farm too. Their lines were forming on the ridge eventually known to historians as Seminary Ridge; the Bliss farm, with Union troops holding it, was a little too close to the ridge for comfort. By 8:00 A.M. Confederate skirmishers advanced in force and drove the Delaware troops back. Now, the Confederates could occupy the Bliss house and barn and seriously harass the Union lines forming just 600 yards from them with their own skirmish lines.

By 9:30 A.M., a larger Union force consisting of ten companies from Ohio and New York regiments advanced upon the Bliss farm from their position in Ziegler's Grove on Cemetery Ridge driving the Confederates back.

The location of the Bliss farm—practically equidistant from each potential main position of the two armies—thus became a whirlpool, drawing more troops from each side to it. New Jersey troops were sent into the mix for the Union side. Union artillery began to arrive and position itself along Cemetery Ridge, rolling into battery and opening fire as they did. About 1:00 P.M., already seven hours into the fighting, there was a lull in the battle over the Bliss Farm.

In the meantime, Confederate commander Robert E. Lee had been reconnoitering the field with his subordinates and determined on a plan to attack the left flank of the enemy beginning from the south in a tactical arrangement known as "*en echelon*." The first attacks by Lieutenant General

Longstreet's Confederates would take place beginning with the far-right end of Lee's line, then additional troops would be advanced to their left, then more to their left and so on.

As Historian Christ noted, "The series of events that occurred on the Bliss Farm following the initiation of Longstreet's attack altered the outcome of the day's engagement."

About 3:00 P.M., Lee's *en echelon* attack began and swept northward, his brigades successively assailing the Union line, driving the Yankees out of Devil's Den, the Peach Orchard, the Wheatfield, from Trostle's Farm and continuing up their lines.

Around 4:00 P.M., Confederates again advanced against the heavy Union skirmish line at the Bliss farm and pushed them back. Using the buildings like a makeshift fortress, the Bliss farm's Confederate occupants could fire southeast toward Pennsylvania skirmishers near the Codori farm and northeast toward Ohio troops on Cemetery Ridge. As well, some Confederates had already advanced from the Bliss farm all the way to the Emmitsburg Road, less than 200 yards from the main Union lines. A bayonet-studded rush of the 8th Ohio Volunteers soon drove them back to the Bliss buildings.

The Bliss farm continued to draw troops from both sides. And now, bigger egos began to get involved. Brigadier General Alexander Hays, commanding the Union troops in and around Zeigler's Grove, being harassed by fire from the Bliss farm, challenged officers around him: "Have you a regiment that will drive them [the Confederates] out?" "Yes, Sir," Colonel Thomas Smyth answered, "the 12th will do it!" and promptly volunteered the 12th New Jersey Regiment. Meanwhile, the troops from Delaware and Pennsylvania, driven back earlier, joined them in their attack on the Virginians and Mississippians now occupying the Bliss farm buildings.

By 6:00 P.M. the New Jerseyans had wrested the Bliss farm from the Confederates, but found themselves in an increasingly untenable spot. Brigadier General Ambrose Wright's entire Confederate brigade and parts of another brigade were advancing as the northernmost section of the main Confederate attack. Seeing this overwhelming assault in motion, the New Jersey troops were forced to withdraw from the Bliss farm leaving it again to the Confederates.

One of the barely recognized but pivotal moments of the Battle of Gettysburg was about to take place. Wright's Brigade had reached the Union line near the spot that would become known as the Copse of Trees—the center of the Union line that Robert E. Lee would covet less than 24 hours later during what would come to be known as Pickett's Charge, the final assault on the Union lines at Gettysburg.

In his official account of his brigade's actions late on the afternoon of July 2, Brigadier General Wright recounts his attack across the Emmitsburg Road, of capturing Union artillery pieces and driving the Union troops from stone walls, over the top of the ridge and into a "rocky gorge on the eastern slope of the heights, and some 80 or 100 yards in rear" of their artillery batteries.

He summed up his situation: "We were now complete masters of the field, having gained the key, as it were, of the enemy's whole line."

But when he looked around, they were alone. The brigade to their right had retired, and the troops on their left, many of which had been fighting for the Bliss farm all day, were completely worn out and unable to support them. Wright had no choice but to withdraw. Later, Lee received the intelligence that Wright had come to within a hair's breadth of breaking through the center of the Union line. Some historians believe it may have been that knowledge that convinced Lee to attempt to crack the Union center the next day, with 12,500 men instead of a single brigade.

But as Wright later told a fellow officer, "The trouble is not in going there, the trouble is to stay there after you get there, for the whole Yankee army is there in a bunch."

According to Christ, "Thus the situation at the Bliss Farm around 6:45 P.M. stymied the Confederate *en echelon* attack."

The pressure from Union units in their rear and to the north disallowed the Confederates in the area to support Wright's Brigade.

Christ concludes the time period from 6:30 to 8:30 P.M., July 2, as "one of the most critical periods of the Battle of Gettysburg." He notes that while Confederates had reached the Union gunners atop East Cemetery Hill fighting hand-to-hand, Confederates attacked up Culp's Hill and entered abandoned Union trenches, halting just a few minutes' advance from the Baltimore Pike, the rear of the Union army and retreat routes. And all along this Cemetery Hill sector, the Union lines had been stripped to their bare bones earlier in the afternoon to bolster their comrades in the fighting farther south.

Some historians like to say that Lee's July 2 afternoon attack "lost momentum," but Christ points out that the fighting at the Bliss farm destroyed whatever spontaneous "pincer" style attack the Confederates might have had beyond Cemetery and Culp's Hills and was the actual cause of the loss of momentum of Lee's *en echelon* attack against the Union line along Cemetery Ridge.

Confederates held the Bliss farm over the night of July 2-3. But by 7:00 A.M., July 3, the Bliss farm caught the attention of Union officers again.

Confederates at the Bliss farm apparently brought it on themselves by being deadly pests with their sharpshooting skills against Union troops in and around Zeigler's Grove. Brigadier General Hays ordered the farmstead retaken.

It was an undersized attack of some 60 men, but armed with rapid-firing, breech-loading Sharps rifles, the 14th Connecticut Infantry hoped with their sophisticated armament to tip the scales in their favor.

Overall Union commander in the area, Major General Winfield S. Hancock, apparently felt the Bliss farm enclave so dangerous to operations that he had ordered it burned. The order was pocketed by Brigadier General Hays, still convinced he could drive the enemy from the farm.

The small contingent from the 14th Connecticut drove the rebels from the barn and house and consolidated in the barn, but Confederate artillery on Seminary Ridge, along with southern riflemen from the re-taken Bliss house, again made the Bliss farm untenable for Union troops.

Around 11:30 A.M., General Hays, after watching the see-saw battle for the Bliss farm go into its second day, determined that Hancock's order to burn what had become a "bone of contention" would be implemented. Hays sent troops to the Bliss farm with the orders and fire-starting materials.

So quickly had the Bliss family left their home that soldiers found Adeline Bliss's bedding materials on the second floor of the house and used them to start the fire; convinced the fire had caught, they sprinted to William Bliss's barn, lighting mounds of hay and straw, then fell back to the main Union lines.

As Christ notes: "...the hopes and dreams of William Bliss and his family were consumed in flames. The buildings—whose walls had been silent witnesses to six years of fond memories and hard work—had sheltered soldiers from such divergent parts of the country as Mississippi and Connecticut, and had withstood approximately thirty hours of shot and shell. They were destroyed in a matter of minutes."

The men who fought so long over the Bliss farm had barely an hour to eat, re-hydrate, and rest. At 1:00 P.M., as smoke from the remains of the farm was still rising, Confederate artillery all along Seminary Ridge roared in the massive cannonade preceding the main Confederate assault on the Union center known to history as Pickett's Charge.

Confederate Colonel E. P. Alexander, in charge of the Confederate bombardment, was painfully aware of the cost to his artillery of wasting ammunition earlier on the skirmish around the Bliss farm. By 3:00 P.M., he was desperately sending messages to his superiors that if they wanted any artillery support for the infantry advance, they must launch it soon: he was running dangerously low on ammunition.

As well, once the attack began, Confederate infantry on the assault's left had to open ranks to pass around the orchard, fences, and still smoldering ruins of the farm, all the while under Union artillery fire and flank fire from the 8th Ohio Infantry.

Christ summed up his subject with numbers and the emotional tragedies, great and small, of the fighting around and destruction of one family's farm and livelihood. While but a "skirmish" in the vast panoply that was the Battle of Gettysburg, the fight for the Bliss farm was brutal. It changed hands at least 10 times during the fighting. "Between sunrise of 2 July and the early afternoon of 3 July, approximately 2,160 Union and 2,310 Confederate soldiers fought around the Bliss Farm, suffering casualties of about 360 and 470 respectively. The Southern troops suffered a slightly higher percentage loss—20% versus 17%."

His description of what happened to the Bliss family points out their unique tragedy: "Of all the civilians that had been directly affected by Lee's Gettysburg Campaign, they were the only ones who had lost nearly everything except for the clothes on their back and what little they were able to haul away."

It is not noted what the Bliss family did in the next four years—probably, somehow, they attempted to gather together enough money to rebuild their farm and lived hand-to-mouth—but by 1867 they were forced to sell their land for a loss and return to Chautauqua County, New York. From there they began the tedious task of attempting to apply for reparations from federal and state governments for the destruction of their private property by the Union Army. Bureaucratic red tape and governmental runarounds outlived both William and Adeline Bliss and they saw not a penny repayment for what the federal forces did to their farm. Their daughter continued petitioning, filing forms, and jumping through hoops until December 1902, when the Senate vetoed a bill authorizing payment for the damages to the Bliss buildings, slamming the door shut permanently.

Though the Bliss Farm is long gone, and the Bliss family's long suffering forgotten, it seems that the psychic remnants of it and some of the men who fought for it, apparently, eerily, still remain.

I received a handwritten letter in the early 1990s—found recently in my "Lost Files"—that tells of an experience that may be attributed to what paranormalists call a "warp" or tear in the fabric of time providing a glimpse into the past.

Many out-of-time sightings of spirits and scenes may be the result of this warp. It seems like time, the thing we live with daily, that we should be most familiar with, is actually very elusive and mysterious. At times it seems to speed up, as in "where did the time go?" or slow down, especially during mundane or tiresome tasks. Ask anyone who has passed the age of 65 about the years gone by: "My, how they've flown."

So, to imagine, during certain states of mind, or in certain special places on this earth, for time to sort of crack open, like a veil being pushed aside, and offer a vision into the past, is not out of the realm of possibilities.

The writer of the letter tells of his trip to Gettysburg, after a traumatic personal experience at home, alone without his family for the first time. He went to visit the Battle Theater on the edge of the fields of Pickett's Charge and was waiting in his car for a downpour to pass. He was looking out at the field to ascertain how tall the grass was for a planned visit the next day to the site of the Bliss Farm. According to his letter, "Looking out I was amazed to see a house and barn in the distance." He thought he had read somewhere that the National Park Service was planning to rebuild a replica of the Bliss Farm buildings. He was impressed at the detail of the huge barn and the trim in the windows of the house, "altogether a great looking place." He was looking forward to visiting the restored Bliss Farm the next day.

The following day he drove along Long Lane to get as close as possible to walk to the reconstruction. "Needless to say, I was shocked to see just the mounds where the house and barn had been." He drove up and down the lane, then returned to the parking lot of the Battle Theater and realized that his view into the fields would have been blocked by trees now there. The day before there had been an opening in the tree line and a clear view into the field to the Bliss Farm.

Having seen a number of episodes of "The Twilight Zone," the popular sci-fi program of the black and white era of television, he admitted he was reluctant to venture out into the field to inspect the site more closely. A script for the show would have had him sucked back into time, perhaps re-fighting the battle, possibly dying a hundred years before he was even born. Instead, he remembered that there was a monument on Hancock Avenue, just a few hundred yards away, that held a bronze sculpture of the Bliss Farm.

Bronze Relief on Monument

Seeing the bronze on the monument to the 12th New Jersey Volunteers was a shock: it was a cast sculpture eerily similar to his vision of the day before, same barn and house, but with soldiers fighting over it. Trying to rationalize the irrational, he remembered reading that the Bliss family was never reimbursed for the destruction of their property by the government forces and that the same government had been doing some excavations at the site of the destroyed property. Perhaps the government's desire to rebuild the farm's structures, coming over a century too late for the Bliss family to benefit from the efforts, had upset the now long-dead family members.

Disappearing structures are not so bizarre in paranormal studies. While compiling stories for my book *Civil War Ghost Trails* (Stackpole Books, 2012), a woman who lived in the vicinity of the battlefields of Manassas in Virginia related an event that happened in her "neighborhood." One night she was driving through the intersection where the famous "Stone House" stands. It is a landmark for both 1st and 2nd Manassas battles, when it became a hospital for the wounded, but predates the Civil War by many decades. It's reputation of being haunted goes back to 1866. The woman was very familiar with the old house having driven past hundreds of times. This time, when she looked for it...it was gone. She almost panicked, wondering what catastrophe had befallen the beloved structure that prompted the National Park Service to tear it down. Returning after her appointment, she decided she would pull over and examine the site for clues as to what happened. Approaching the intersection, she was astounded: the old stone house was still there, apparently re-appearing out of nowhere.

Later, among friends, she reluctantly related her experience, waiting for the teasing and jeers. All were solemn until one spoke up, seemingly for the others: Yes, the disappearance of the stone house had happened to him, too, as well as its re-appearance just a few hours later.

In November 2007, I received an e-mail from a man and his wife from Indiana. Just a week before they had been visiting the Gettysburg Battlefield. It was late afternoon and they decided to have an early dinner at about 4:30. It had been raining on and off when they pulled into the parking lot for the former "General Pickett's Buffet," which was in the building that housed the Gettysburg Battle Theater. His wife said, "What the heck is that guy doing standing out in that field in the rain?" She looked at her husband who glanced into the field but couldn't see anything. When she turned back, the man in the field was gone.

Her husband gave her a sarcastic remark as to the existence of the man and she became adamant about her vision. She said he had his head bowed with his back to her and wore a blue coat with blue pants. Her husband asked for a little more description and was told that the color was definitely not navy blue. He off-handedly remarked that she must have seen a ghost because there was no one around and no cars pulling away from the area. A visit to the National Park Service Museum gave her a glimpse at the colors she had seen the apparition wearing, as did a reenactor out on the field who was kind enough to pose for a photo with his back to her, solidifying in her mind that what she had seen briefly was an accurate image of what was reality. One final question the husband had in his letter to me was, had I heard any reports of sightings on the northern edge of the field of battle near the area of General Pickett's Buffet? It took a few more years to get a documented answer, but in 2010, it came unsolicited in another e-mail.

A man from New Jersey who was visiting the area of the Bliss Farm during Remembrance Weekend that year was compelled to drop me an e-mail. He and a friend went out to the farm site after dark with their cameras, looking for ghosts, but "fully expecting to NOT see any because I wanted to." He described the night as clear with no ground fog to obscure his view. While walking along the fence he got what he described as "an extremely weird feeling and the hair on my neck felt like it was standing up." Rightfully taking this as a sign of ghostly activity, he got his camera ready to shoot as did his friend. He aimed along the fence, but in spite of the battery being fully charged, the camera failed to take a picture. Nothing worked, not even the viewfinder. He brought the camera down to look at it and it clicked. Still, he saw nothing in the viewfinder. But when he looked up along the fence, there was a figure not twenty feet in front of him.

He described the man as "in full color, blurry, but detailed enough to make things out." He saw that he was a young Confederate soldier, dressed in the butternut uniform so commonly worn at Gettysburg, crouched down with his musket aimed toward the Union lines. Suddenly, "he saw me, acted very startled and surprised, stood abruptly, looked me right in the eyes, inverted his musket in surrender and began to approach me!"

Describing exactly the definition of an "intelligent" or "interactive" haunting he wrote, "He clearly saw ME and was responding to ME!"

The fact that this happened during Remembrance Weekend would cause me to attribute the case to a reenactor "playing" ghost to freak out any tourist who ventures out on the battlefield. But then he added something that reenactors have not been able to accomplish:

"Because of HIS response, I too was startled, but began to approach him and he vanished."

He continued with his recalled description, that the soldier was missing his kepi, had black leather "cross-belts" (which would have been his cartridge box belt and a black Union tarred haversack—often taken by Confederates from dead Union soldiers), that his eyes were dark and appeared "tall and gawky."

As for back up to his vision, his friend saw nothing. He had his head turned in the other direction for the time the spirit was visible. But the witness was so sure of what he had seen that he planned another trip back to the Bliss Farm site, wearing the same clothing, including his Union reproduction kepi with the 2nd Corps insignia, so that perhaps the same "intelligent" spirit will recognize him.

I have not heard from him about his second visit to the site of the Bliss Farm and the savage battle that whirled around it, both of which now have vanished like the spirits seen there and the family who once lived there…where dreams came to die.

HELL NIGHT

Time does not exist—we invented it. Time is what the clock says. The distinction between the past, present and future is only a stubbornly persistent illusion

—Albert Einstein

Combat in the American Civil War was a descent into Hell. If you were ordered to attack the enemy, the deafening blast of his cannons becomes the stomach-churning overture to the hailstorm of hundreds of .58 caliber, soft lead minié balls flying at 900 feet per second, all seemingly aimed right at you. Some bullets hit nearby friends, who scream or choke or swear or silently slump to the hard rocky ground as you continue your insane march toward their fiery source.

Defending a position, you crouch behind some inadequate, hastily assembled breastwork of fence rails for your attackers to get closer. His artillery has already been firing at you, shells bursting overhead, ripping great pieces of comrades' bodies and flinging them, or simply making those comrades vanish in a great blast of heat and iron and smoke. If you are lucky, it is only *their* blood and internal organs that are splattered violently upon you; unlucky, and it's your own body parts gouged out and strewn across the field.

And that was in the daylight.

If you must fight at night, the horrors and fear are amplified. While you may be spared the horror of the *sight* of the butchery, still, through the darkness came the screams, gagging, howls, curses, begging, and groans. Attack in the dark and you tripped over God-knows-what—a branch, fallen log, fallen friend, a hand weakly grasping for help, a piece of meat that once was the leg of a man. You hear the hoarse, shouted orders, but whose they are you do not know. You cannot see the colors—the soul of the unit that meant life or death—to follow and so stumble forward, until there's the blinding flare of an exploding line of muskets or artillery and the sickening thud of soft lead into flesh. Then, at best, you fire at musket flashes, hoping they belonged to the enemy and not comrades.

Fortunately, night fighting in the American Civil War was relatively rare mainly because communication to coordinate attacks largely depended upon line-of-sight and sound. Long-distance field communication techniques in the years before the Civil War consisted of drums, reflected sunlight, fires, smoke, flag signaling and, of course, human couriers who sometimes made it through alive to deliver their messages, but sometimes didn't, vital orders lost in the fog of war. The wired telegraph and Morse code came into use in the 1840s and were used toward the end of the Civil War in battlefield communications when the sappers had time to put up poles and string wire. Gettysburg, however, was such a quick and savage battle that telegraphic field communications between fighting units was never attempted.

Wireless radio communication was decades into the future. Portable wireless field communications, and miniaturized, long-distance communications for the individual soldier, even further ahead.

So, directing troop movements, exact coordination of attacks, and identifying friend or foe was always problematic— and often lethal to your own troops—during night operations in the 1860s.

At Gettysburg, after their initial defeat on July 1, 1863, the Union Army was driven to the high ground south of the town, into a line running from Culp's Hill, curving across Cemetery Hill, straightening to run down Cemetery Ridge, eventually to end—after fighting for it—on Little Round Top. Confederate commander Robert E. Lee, after scouting the fish hook-shaped line of battle the Federal troops occupied, formulated his battle plan for July 2.

He reasoned that if his troops could coordinate attacks upon each end of the Union line simultaneously, it would nullify some of the advantages of the enemy having an "interior" line. Occupying both ends of their line in combat would leave them unable to send troops from one flank of their line rapidly to help the other.

The key word to this strategy was "simultaneously." In other words, coordinated Confederate attacks on Culp's and Cemetery Hills on the Union Army's right flank and the area near Little Round Top on its left.

Problems arose almost immediately. Lieutenant General James Longstreet's men were to be in place early on July 2, but Longstreet was told to keep his men from being seen by Union signalmen on Little Round Top. He reached a point in his march where his column was exposed and had to re-trace his march route and find lower ground along which to hide his movements. The result was that his troops were not in position to launch their July 2 assault until between 3:00 and 4:00 P.M.

Meantime, Lieutenant General Richard S. Ewell, on the other end of the Confederate line, was told to wait until he heard Longstreet's guns to the south, then launch his attack. After waiting all day for Longstreet's guns, a courier came from Lee changing the orders to *creating a diversion, but developing a full attack if practicable.* Ewell's troops lost valuable daylight, but got their assault on Culp's and East Cemetery Hills in motion by around 8:00 P.M., resulting in two night-time battles for the hills.

I have chronicled some of the night fighting on Culp's Hill in *Gettysburg's Hidden, Haunted, Hotspots,* and wrote about it in other volumes of the *Ghosts of Gettysburg* series and emphasized how close the Confederates came to breaking through the Union line. Hopefully, I also gave an impression of the difficulty of fighting at night up the thickly wooded slope of Culp's Hill. At about the same time as the Culp's Hill attack, however, another Confederate assault was making its way towards the barren, east-facing slope of Cemetery Hill.

According to the late Gregory A. Coco, in his monumental work, *A Strange and Blighted Land, Gettysburg: The Aftermath of a Battle* what is now known as East Cemetery Hill was called "Raffensperger Hill," named after Peter and Rebecca Raffensperger, the wartime owners of the land. Before the battle, the slope rolled evenly down to a peaceful, undulating valley, reminding one of fox-hunting country.

But, there, in the waning daylight hours of July 2, 1863, the game to be hunted this night was human.

Brigadier General Harry T. Hays' Louisiana Brigade was lined up along Winebrenner's Run which ran generally east and west along the low ground near where LeFever Street is located today, but now drains from below ground, under the parking lots for the Gettysburg school complex. Hoke's Brigade was closer to the Culp Farm's spring house, according to Historian Harry W. Pfanz in his book, *Gettysburg: Culp's Hill and Cemetery Hill.* Soon after the fighting began on Culp's Hill, the decision was made to turn the "demonstration" into a full-scale assault, including attacks on the north and western slopes of Cemetery Hill, creating pressure on three sides of the key position.

But the attacks on Cemetery Hill from the north and west never materialized; the Union artillery on those parts of Cemetery Hill and their excellent fields of fire dissuaded that part of the Confederate assault. So, the Yankees had no distractions from the north and west slopes as Hays' and Hoke's men assaulted East Cemetery Hill on their own.

Hays' Louisianans marched in battle lines from out of the depression of Winebrenner's Run, passed through a brickyard with their right generally following Brickyard Lane (now named Wainwright Avenue), acting as the hinge to a "swinging gate" the left regiments of the brigade would become.

There was a stone wall that ran from the Baltimore Pike eastward over East Cemetery Hill to end on Brickyard Lane.

Behind that wall and facing north was placed the 107th Ohio. Several shifts in position brought the 107th Ohio down the hill, closer to the bottom. Extending its line and angling back along the Lane was the 25th Ohio. The rest of the Union troops were positioned behind the stone fence that stretched along Brickyard Lane at the base of Raffensperger Hill, later known as East Cemetery Hill. All the while, darkness was creeping over the battlefield.

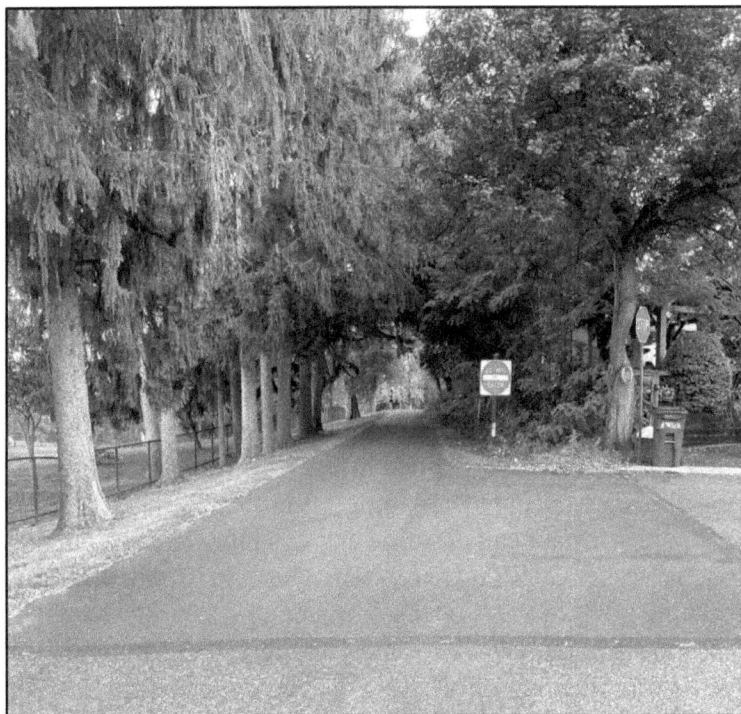

North Entrance to Wainwright Avenue

Fast-forward, same spot, 146 years later:

November 2009. Val and Tony Capone, brothers from Maryland, who are avid Civil War aficionados, were visiting Gettysburg. As well as enjoying the history of Gettysburg, they are also interested in the paranormal aspects and decided to take a late-night walk along Baltimore Street towards town with their nephew Kenny. On a whim, they detoured right on Le Fever Street and stopped where Wainwright Avenue intersects it. Val admitted they had no real plan, other than to take a brisk night-time walk. Tony, Val, and Kenny had never been to that area, even in the daylight. As Val put it, "We figured we would walk a few blocks south towards East Cemetery Hill. Turns out, we wouldn't make it very far."

It was a clear cold night with not much of a moon. Anyone who has walked past the old Gettysburg Athletic Stadium down Wainwright in the evening will understand how dark it can get away from the streetlights, under glowering trees on either side of the avenue casting the area into shadows no matter what time of day or night. They passed on their left the hollow containing the athletic stadium and the bronze statue of "The Warrior"— Gettysburg High School's namesake Native-American mascot. As they continued their night-time stroll off the road along the grassy area to the left of the avenue, they could barely see the ground beneath their feet. (This was before the new stadium was built and the fences were in a different position.)

Val wrote, "We slowly walked maybe 150 yards or so and we all stopped because we felt an odd change in the air. It suddenly felt like we stepped into a vacuum. I began hearing the sounds of a campsite some 50-60 yards ahead of us. I could hear what I can describe as mess kits, tin cups, buckles on harnesses, etc. Activity somewhere in front of us, but nothing at all to see. For the moment, at least."

At this point, I have to interject something. In over fifty years of collecting ghost stories, I have learned that certain people are better eyewitnesses to paranormal events. I've found that nurses, doctors, and police are often good witnesses because they are professionally trained observers. To this group I must add certain military types.

From 1983 to 1987 Val had served in an artillery fire direction unit in the 7th Infantry Division, working his way up to section chief. Their specialty was small unit night operations. He trained with the 82nd and 101st Airborne Divisions as well as the Marines. Their unit motto was "Masters of the Night."

His training took him to Korea for cold weather training, Panama for jungle training, Hawaii, Guam, "under terrible simulated combat scenarios…I was in the field somewhere over 100 days a year. Intensive night training courses; night air mobile operations (moved frequently by Blackhawk helicopters.) *We were a specially trained unit for night operations and were taught observation techniques that allowed us to detect and identify forces, judge direction and distance, navigate by map/compass, etc.* [Emphasis added.] We didn't have all the fancy optics and lasers they carry today. And night vision goggles wrecked your 'night vision' when you took them off."

Back in time to July 2, 1863, around 8:00 P.M., in the same area where the three men walked:

Keep in mind that all times reported in Civil War accounts refer to local time. There was no Daylight Savings Time in the summer back then, so by 8:00 P.M., darkness was rapidly closing in on the troops both attacking and defending the base of East Cemetery Hill. Although vaguely aware that something was going on in the rolling fields to the east, the Union soldiers along Brickyard Lane at the base of the hill probably weren't aware they were going to be attacked until they heard, out in front of their line, their own skirmishers firing, then seeing them falling back towards them in the dusk.

The right of Hays' line, according to historian Pfanz, probably advanced along Brickyard Lane for some 250 yards; the left of the line began to wheel right, over the hill where the school buildings now stand, to eventually come into contact with Hoke's Brigade, marching from near the Culp Farmhouse, both lines then able to strike the Federals face-to-face. The brigade's namesake and former commander, Robert F. Hoke had been wounded at Chancellorsville in May 1863, so the brigade was commanded at Gettysburg by Colonel Isaac E. Avery who chose to ride his horse into the battle.

On top of East Cemetery Hill, Union artillery began firing at what they could see in the gathering darkness of the advancing Confederates. Steven's Battery, on the far right of the Union line, had the best vantage point, on the left flank of the attacking Confederate lines. Earlier in the day they had measured distances to landmarks with a special instrument and fired some test rounds to know the range to fire effectively if attacked from that quarter. Cooper's Battery, on top of East Cemetery Hill, fought-out because of an afternoon artillery duel with Latimer's Battery on Benner's Hill, was relieved by Rickett's Battery.

Forward in time again to November 2009:

So, Val, Tony and Kenny were now walking unknowingly in the historical footsteps of Hays' Brigade as they continued into the inky darkness ahead toward the sounds being made by invisible soldiers. We know a little about the soldiers who once manned the wall toward which they were headed: The 107th Ohio was recruited from Cleveland and Cuyahoga County in northern Ohio and was sometimes called the "5th German Regiment" since over 70 per cent of them were German immigrants. To their right was the 25th Ohio whose line ran along the same wall facing north towards town for about half its length; then it was "refused"—military parlance for "bent back"—along Brickyard Lane. The 25th was organized at Camp Chase in Columbus, Ohio, and had participated in at least nine battles before Gettysburg.

Val continues his narrative as events progressed along Wainwright Avenue:

"As we talked among ourselves and tried to figure out what was happening, in the distance, towards what looked like some small trees, we began to see what appeared to be small, white/grayish forms ahead of us in the direction of the campsite sounds." Tony described what he saw at a distance of about 50 yards as looking like white plastic grocery bags floating in the breeze. "We were trying to come up with an explanation because it was getting creepy. At some point while we were watching these 4 or 5 things getting larger and larger in size, we got the impression that they were actually getting closer. I would say they got to around 4-5 feet in height but very narrow, maybe 10 inches wide. Now I was sure these things were moving straight towards us." Val admits, "We got spooked and retreated to the 'safety' of the lights in the parking lot."

Ohio Monument on Wainwright Avenue

Let me explain something. These are not the type of men who would retreat from much of anything. First, both are large men, over six feet, two inches each. Tony looks like he could have played defensive lineman for the Baltimore Ravens; Val, maybe a tight end. They grew up in Baltimore, sons of a Baltimore policeman, and ran a business in Fells Point for a number of years, facing down the inherent, sometimes life-threatening dangers working in that city entails.

Kenny, however, had had enough and walked back to the hotel room. "Tony and I decided to head back to the same spot" [the area they had just left.] Thinking about it for a few minutes, Val's curiosity got the better of him. "What I experienced was so incredible I needed to see if it would happen again. It did, and much more."

Night, July 2, 1863:
The lay of the land and darkness protected the Confederates for a while, and the closer they got to Union line on Brickyard Lane, the less they would have to contend with the Union artillery, since the cannoneers wouldn't fire into the backs of their own men.

In spite of the deadly flank fire from Steven's Battery, within minutes Confederates reached the base of the hill, fired volleys from the covering darkness, then leapt the wall near the center of the Union line where hand-to-hand fighting eventually stretched along the lane. On the Union left, there was a gap between the 25th and 75th Ohio regiments, and the Confederates exploited it, forcing the Buckeye units to retreat up the hill. In the now nearly total darkness, the fighting turned to chaos, the men using bayonets and muskets as cudgels and not knowing whether the muzzle-flashes they were firing at were friend or foe. One sergeant from the 25th Ohio recalled the enemy charging *downhill* from his left. The 107th was apparently ordered to fall back up the hill to the artillery battery and defend it to the last man.

November 2009, Val continues his narrative:
"We retraced our footsteps and arrived back at the same place. Standing in the darkness, I could feel that odd sensation again. It took about 5 minutes or so before we saw those white forms ahead of us. They started small and grew

larger, same as before. This time I had the impression that a small team was being sent out to see what we wanted. As we're facing towards the south alongside Wainwright, I could clearly see East Cemetery Hill slightly off to the right. Not having seen this area in the daytime I was at a disadvantage in trying to figure the lay of the land. From what I could tell there was a patch of trees directly ahead of us maybe 50-60 yards away. Beyond that in the general direction of Culps Hill, perhaps a few hundred yards of open terrain which appeared lighter in color. It was about 100 yards or so to the base of East Cemetery Hill. There were only a few trees along the other side of Wainwright Ave. and the area appeared especially dark.

The memory of what happened next has stayed with me since that night."

Night, July 2, 1863:

A little farther down Brickyard Lane from the gap where the withdrawal of the 107th and 25th Ohio took place, the 75th Ohio and 17th Connecticut held. According to Pfanz, "…on its left the 75th had the flank protection of the wall that led uphill to Wiedrick's battery and a clump of trees that would probably have impeded the attackers." By now it was so dark that the Confederates could be seen illuminated only by their musket flashes. On came the rebels in this sector until they too clashed hand-to-hand with the Yankees. One captain from the 17th grabbed a Louisianan and dragged him over the wall, his personal prisoner. But Confederates surged through the Brickyard Lane line and up the slope toward the cannons.

Wainwright Avenue Entrance
(Bottom of East Cemetery Hill)

Near this time, Colonel Avery was shot in the neck and, mortally wounded, fell from his horse. The grandson of a Revolutionary War officer and one of 16 children, three of whom would die in the Civil War, in his last moments on this earth, wanted his father to know something and scribbled a pencil message on a scrap of paper: "Tell my father I died with my face to the enemy." The note, stained with his blood as he wrote it on the battlefield of Gettysburg, is today a revered possession in the Archives of the state of North Carolina.

Meantime, the Confederates were taking the fight up the hill; their objectives were the cannons at the summit, to either capture them and turn them on the enemy troops, or to spike them—a procedure to make them inoperable so they couldn't be used against the Confederates anymore.

The Louisiana men got to Wiedrich's guns, the farthest north of the several batteries upon the crest. A rebel color-bearer's silhouette was seen against the skyline atop one of the guns waving a flag as a rallying point for the men coming up the hill. Too valuable a target to let go, within seconds he was shot down, only to be replaced by another. He too, crumpled to the ground. An officer picked up the flag and climbed upon the gun, but was shot in the flag-bearing arm; he switched hands, waved the colors a few more times, then was knocked off the gun, a minié ball in his chest.

Cannon Line on East Cemetery Hill
Photo Courtesy of Luke Butcher

Another son of the South got to one of the guns and threw himself over the muzzle shouting to the Germans making up the Yankee gun crew, "I take command of this gun!" The number 4 man holding the firing lanyard shouted in German, "Thou shalt have them!" jerked the lanyard and blew the Confederate apart.

Rickett's Battery, the next in line to the south of Wiedrich's had their left section—two guns—over-run by

Confederates who tried to spike the guns. But driving the soft lead spike into the primer-hole, then slamming the ramrod down the bore to bend the spike so as to make it impossible to remove without special skills, proved to be too complicated when fighting for their lives.

The Army Manual for Artillery during the Civil War recommends to the officers to remove all personal weapons from the artillerists—meaning sabers and pistols—before going into battle, so that they will "stick to their guns"—use the cannon to fight—rather than attempt to save themselves individually. So "hand-to-hand combat" between infantry and artillerists took on a violent and savage character. While infantry fired their rifled-muskets at point blank range then used the bayonet or their musket as a club, artillerists used rammers, hand-spikes (the club-shaped wooden devices used to turn and aim the cannon), fists and stones to drive off their attackers. In one gruesome case, a Union lieutenant pounded a Confederate in the head with a nearby rock, grabbed a musket and shot him, then clubbed him with the musket.

According to Pfanz, the 107th Ohio had retreated up the hill to behind Wiedrich's Battery at the top of the hill. They were by now somewhat disorganized, but so were the Confederates swarming around the guns. Lieutenant Peter F. Young of the 107th saw the color-bearer of the 8th Louisiana rallying some of his comrades with the flag he held. Young ordered a volley to be fired at the group which broke them up. He ran to the man who had picked up the flag, shot him with his pistol and took the flag. Young himself was shot on his way back to his men. A Confederate tried to take the flag back but was sabered by another Ohio lieutenant, and the colors of the 8th Louisiana went to the 107th Ohio.

Then, one of those strange, unexplainable lulls in battle descended on the hill. In his official report, (from the *Official Records of the War of the Rebellion*), Hays wrote that "A quiet of several minutes now ensued." With the Union artillery silenced, the Confederates thought perhaps the battle was over, that they had won, sent back for reinforcements to hold the position, and began to re-organize. But a few saw through the smoke and darkness a body of infantry approaching. When the unknown troops got to within 100 yards, according to Hays, "a line was discovered before us, from the whole length of which a simultaneous fire was delivered." Having been warned that some of their own troops might be advancing from that direction, Hays did not return the fire.

Hays' men were fired upon again, then again. Clearly something was wrong, so the Confederates returned fire and halted the unidentified attackers. It appeared through the smoke, haze and darkness that more troops were behind them, so Hays rallied his men behind the stone wall at the bottom of the hill. From there they fell back another 75 yards to a fence.

Pfanz identifies the troops who attacked Hays as New Yorkers from Krzyzanowski's Brigade, sent by General O. O. Howard himself to stem the rebel tide on East Cemetery Hill. More fresh Union troops had moved across the Baltimore Pike and helped drive the exhausted Louisianans back to the bottom of the hill. Drawn by the racket from the fighting over the guns, Carroll's Union Brigade from the Second Corps was also pulled into the fray. They moved through the batteries and pushed the other Confederates from their disorganized, unsupported occupation down the hill until they reached the wall along Brickyard Lane.

From the darkness to their left, the Yankees of Carroll's Brigade in the lane, took fire from behind the wall. The colonel from the 14th Indiana shouted for identification from their antagonists who called out they were "Union," but continued firing. The colonel sent the 7th West Virginia to his left to drive them away.

Hays waited for Gordon's Georgians to reinforce his troops. When they didn't come, Hays went looking for them and found them in his old position not moving to support him. It was 10

P.M. Hays wisely led his men back to the approximate position they had held when his dusk attack began.

Back to Val's account, November, 2009:

"Tony and I were occupied by the sight of these objects approaching us from the front. I was feeling antsy and I was ready to head back to the hotel. I admit I really didn't want to turn my back on whatever was in front of us. I was very uncomfortable. At about that time and slightly off to the right, some movement caught our attention. Coming down the north slope of East Cemetery Hill were the same small grayish-type forms that quickly grew into what I will describe as 5 or 6 full-body apparitions in full combat gear. They almost glowed in a grayish, off-white color. On the Hill, they started in a group and then one behind the other, they fell into a single-file line, each about 10 yards apart. As they reached the base of the hill, I could clearly see these were the image of civil war-era troops. They moved at a run holding their muskets in front. I turned to my left to ask my brother if he was seeing the same thing. But he was already halfway to the parking lot. After muttering something that I couldn't make out, he took off. I stayed, mesmerized by what was happening. The apparitions eventually moved along side of me but on the other side of Wainwright Ave. They were no more than 30 yards away. They were clearly visible against the darkness of the hillside. Greyish white in appearance, in uniform and wearing what I knew as the kepi cap with their muskets in hand, backpack, etc. All of this happened in less than a minute when I suddenly realized I was standing alone in the dark, feeling like my ears were plugged, watching something that shouldn't be there. I was overcome by a great deal of fear. Up to that point I had been fighting the urge to run but something changed in me and I felt this panic type of fear. I met my brother at the parking lot and nervously looked over my shoulder on the walk all the way back to the hotel.

"Early the next morning I returned to the same location with my wife. I wanted to see it in daylight. As we made our way to the spot where everything happened, I was shocked. Nothing looked the same. Even the landscape and features didn't match what I saw 6 hours earlier. And these were differences that I could not account for simply because of darkness. The path we walked the night before would have taken us within 20 yards of a large scoreboard and Native American totem. We could not have missed these things, but they were not there the night before. Less than 100 yards away, down Wainwright was a dense tree line of fully grown, mature trees. It wasn't there the night before. And the grove of trees I was seeing in daylight at the base of East Cemetery Hill would have at least partly obscured what I clearly saw the night before. The grove couldn't have been there either.

"I don't know what we stepped into that night. I can't explain what we experienced."

So, what was it Val, Tony and Kenny experienced? From the records gathered by eminent historian Harry W. Pfanz and from the official report of Brigadier General Harry T. Hays, I have come to realize that there was a lot more activity at the Ohioans end of the Union line that ran along Brickyard Lane—Wainwright Avenue—than I'd realized, between the Louisiana Tigers advancing along the Lane, to their eventual retreat in the dark, along that same route.

That retreat of the Confederates is the most logical thing Val and his brother could have seen that night. But the problem is, there was nothing *logical* about it.

What Val and Tony saw happened 146 years and five months before they saw it. The only possible explanation is not a normal one, but a paranormal one.

Was it a so-called warp in time they experienced where a "rip" in the fabric of time occurs and we, the living, can actually see into the past, into the world of the now-dead? Or did time—which is not necessarily always linear—circle back upon itself for just those few minutes and reveal what once had occurred there? Or were the intense energies expended by the participants of the battle over a century before been so focused that they left an indelible remnant record on the very earth where they fought; what some paranormalists call "place memory"? Or, for some as yet unknown reason, were the dead allowed to cross over into the land of the living by adjusting their light frequency so as to be seen?

Answer those questions and you will answer why Gettysburg is so rife with hauntings. As Albert Einstein once observed: *Everything is energy and that is all there is to it. Match the frequency of the reality you want and you cannot help but get that reality. It can be no other way. This is not philosophy. This is physics.*

HARVESTING SOULS IN THE WHEATFIELD

...reckless front attacks, where highest valor was deepest loss; buffetings on bloody angles; butchering in slaughter pens...morning reports at last not called for, and when we asked explanation our superiors answered—confidentially, lest it seem disloyal: "Because the country would not stand it, if they knew."

—Joshua L. Chamberlain, *Passing of the Armies.*

When I worked for the National Park Service, we would quote the number 620,000 as the number of dead men slaughtered from a nation of, according to the 1860 census, 31.5 million souls, in the four years of the American Civil War. "More Americans died in the American Civil War than in all the wars since, added together," we would say to usually horrified listeners. It turns out, we were probably, inadvertently, lying to the American public.

Because of the National Park Service Historians' pristine reputations for accuracy, I remember vividly the day I read that another historian, David Hacker from Binghamton University in New York analyzed, in addition to the military records, the census records of 1860 and 1870, and came up with an estimate of military dead from the Civil War as between 650,000 and 850,000 with the most likely number of 750,000.

From my studies, I understood that only using the military records would not produce an accurate estimate of the deaths caused by the American Civil War. First, accurate keeping of Military Records was far into the future; soldiers were not even issued identification tags ("dog tags") by their respective governments. "Graves Registration" units were non-existent; most burials were done hastily and partially as the armies left the scene of battle quickly and locals were left to clean up. Many soldiers died along retreat routes, left by the side of the road or buried on private property. Union soldiers were usually disinterred later from battlefields, their remains gathered in new "National Cemeteries." Confederate "enemy" dead at Gettysburg were not exhumed until the early 1870s. Even when Southerners were determined to bring their boys home, it was hap-hazard. Battles were large and small and far ranging and graves unmarked. Markers were often pencil on wood boards, proclaiming "23 reb dead." Before long, the wooden markers were knocked over by grazing animals, seasons came and went, grass and weeds grew, and gravesites lost.

And, per the quote by Major General Joshua L. Chamberlain above, toward the end of the war, record keeping of the dead, wounded and missing was virtually suspended to hide the true cost of the war from the civilian population.

So, the figures arrived at by Hacker were truly shocking to me, almost a third more having died in the war than I had originally thought. Consider also that the country was one-tenth its present population. In other words, like they often do when explaining how much the cost of something in the past was "in today's dollars," make the 850,000 dead 8,500,000.

Can you imagine what the country would say if a current war cost us eight and a half million young men—and young women—in just four years?

So, perhaps all our numerical statistics should be taken with the proverbial grain of salt. Especially since the "fudge factor" is 200,000, give or take. But once again, we must force ourselves to remember that it is not just a number. It is 200,000—to add to the original 600,000—human beings: men and boys with wives, mothers, fathers, brothers and sisters, and potential descendants who would have lived in our time, to become individuals in our families, to have contributed to our culture, now. Unborn, un-named, unknown. Those men who died because of the Civil War, as many as 850,000, surrendered up so much more than just their lives. They gave their future generations.

And that is the curse of all wars on humankind, that so much more is sacrificed than is ever realized.

But wars don't just happen. Politicians get us into them, sometimes by their blundering, sometimes on purpose, for whatever reason they might have. Politicians have been a part of starting wars since countries began waging them.

And the biggest curse of all is laid on those who start them.

With that in mind, the ultimate cost of human military conflict, the morbid debate rages: Which of the three days at Gettysburg was the bloodiest?

July 3, seems to be the first guess in everybody's mind, as the bloodiest day of the battle, having been the infamous day of Pickett's Charge, the attack that is legendary for its fifty minutes of savagery and destruction of human life. No doubt, the rapidity of men being shot down was enough to scorch the day's images into everyone's brain. In addition, there were the casualties on the Union side defending against Pickett's Charge, casualties from the two-hour cannonade preceding the actual assault, and the wounded, missing and dead from the cavalry fighting at East Cavalry Battlefield, the Battle at Fairfield, and Farnsworth's Charge.

If you add casualties from the July 3, early morning fighting on Culp's Hill, the figures grow. Jeffry D. Wert in his comprehensive volume Gettysburg Day Three writes that the assault of Pickett's Division cost the Confederate cause 2,653 casualties; the rest of the participating Confederates of Pettigrew and Trimble suffered even more, totaling around 5,400. To illustrate the difficulty in determining casualties in Civil War combat, the National Park Service has quoted "two-thirds" of the original 12,500 men in the grand charge on July 3—approximately 8,300—became casualties. The other battles that day would bring the totals up slightly, but even if you take the high figures from the NPS, the casualties are still lower than even July 1.

July 1, although hard-fought and costly, is hardly ever considered for producing a large number of casualties. But author David Martin gives the Union and Confederate casualties for the first day's fight at 14,992; Harry Pfanz, in his book on July 1, totals the combined casualties at 15,500.

Let's finally look at July 2. Harry Pfanz in his book Gettysburg: The Second Day, chronicling the fighting on just the southern end of the battlefield wrote this: "It had been a costly three hours for both armies." He figured that the three attacking Confederate divisions lost some 6,000 officers and men killed, wounded, and missing. Sickles' two divisions from the Third Corps lost in killed, wounded and missing about 4,211. Union Second Corps casualties, defending the line just north of Sickles, lost 2,800 and the Fifth Corps, fighting to save the extreme southern end of the Union line suffered 2,187 casualties, most on July 2. The total Union casualties for the fighting, Pfanz figures are about 9,000.

So, the fighting just for the afternoon of July 2, cost both armies about 15,000 men.

Of course, July 2 fighting also included the battle for Culps' and Cemetery Hills. In his companion book for the fighting on July 2, (Gettysburg: Culps' Hill and Cemetery Hill), Pfanz lists Confederate losses fighting for Culps' Hill at 1,823 (not including three Confederate Brigades that also fought in the battle) and Union losses for the Twelfth Corps at 1,082 for a total of 2,905 casualties to be added to the 15,000 for a total of nearly 18,000 casualties.

So, July 2, with the drawn-out fighting on Culp's Hill, the Confederate sunset attacks upon East Cemetery Hill, and the Confederates massive en echelon assaults along Cemetery Ridge, from Little Round Top, through Devil's Den, the

Triangular Field, the Wheatfield, the Peach Orchard, stretching nearly to the Copse of Trees (to be made famous the next day during Pickett's Charge) would probably rank as the bloodiest day of the three-day battle.

And much of the bloodshed of nearly Biblical proportions was brought on by the tactical maneuverings of Major General Daniel Sickles.

Sickles was not a trained soldier; he was a politician. He never attended West Point or even a military academy. He had a little pre-war experience as an officer in a New York Militia unit. When the Civil War broke out, he raised a regiment and was appointed its colonel probably because of his name recognition. Before he had even been in a battle, he was made brigadier general. Political wrangling in Washington caused him to miss part of the Peninsula Campaign in the spring 1862, but after working his many political contacts, he participated throughout the rest of the spring and part of the summer in the fighting on the Virginia Peninsula in command of New York's Excelsior Brigade. President Lincoln, himself, in January 1863, raised Sickles to Major General and Major General Joseph Hooker appointed Sickles commander of the Army of the Potomac's Third Corps, a meteoric rise for someone untrained in the military arts.

At Gettysburg, his Third Corps was placed by commanding general George G. Meade as a southern extension of the Union Second Corps line along Cemetery Ridge.

Confederate commander Robert E. Lee, after observing the enemy position on July 2, formulated his plan to attack the Union line on Cemetery Ridge from the southwest en echelon, one brigade after another, hitting the enemy's line like a wave crashing along a slanted shoreline, keeping the whole line busy so Union troops could not be maneuvered to relieve any one beleaguered section. During the morning and early afternoon of July 2, Confederate Major General James Longstreet marched his troops into position for the attack.

After a half-hour bombardment of the Union line, Longstreet's men swept from their position on Seminary Ridge.

But a few hours before Longstreet's attack, Sickles decided he was unsatisfied with his position along Cemetery Ridge and marched his entire Third Army Corps out to the west, away from the rest of the Union line to the Emmitsburg Road, all without orders.

His line was centered roughly on the crossroad formed by the Emmitsburg Road and the road to Millersville where a peach orchard and farmer Wentz's house stood, the area now commemorated famously as The Peach Orchard. At that point, Sickles' line bent back to his right along the Emmitsburg Road, and to his left roughly along the eastern extension of the Millersville Road, now known as The Wheatfield Road, eventually anchoring his left flank in a massive jumble of boulders known locally as the Devil's Den.

The inverted "V"-shaped line created several problems for Union commander George G. Meade. First, Sickles' line was not long enough to re-connect to the rest of the Union Army: Sickles right flank had a gap between it and the Union line on Cemetery Ridge. Just as critical, his left flank failed to reach the high ground on Little Round Top. As well, a "V" shaped line means that projectiles fired at one side of the "V" may fall into the rear of the other side.

Hot-tempered Meade vented his disapproval to Sickles who offered to pull his lines back, but it was too late. Longstreet's Confederate veterans began their assault along the south end of the Union line and ran right into Sickles' men.

On Sickles' left, some of Longstreet's advance simply by-passed the Union soldiers in Devil's Den while others occupied the Yankees there and in the Triangular Field. The southern soldiers who got around Devil's Den advanced over Big Round Top, eventually clashing with Lieutenant Colonel Joshua Chamberlain's 20th Maine, who had just established their position on the slopes of Little Round Top. After serious fighting, the Confederates were driven back.

As that battle was dying down, Confederate troops by-passed Union artillery in the Peach Orchard and advanced past the Rose Farm. Before them lay a once-serene (as recently as the day before) twenty-six acre ripening field of wheat owned by John Rose.

There's a modern interpretive sign at the Wheatfield that calls it the Maelstrom of Death. Actually, it was more like a whirlpool—as one contemporary Park Ranger has called it—drawing units into the swirling, back and forth battles that made up the fighting.

During my Park Ranger days, when a visitor to Gettysburg National Military Park asked about the fighting in the Wheatfield, almost every ranger I knew would come up with some excuse not to go into detail about the battle there. I finally asked my superiors, why, and was told that the fighting was so confused with so many units being thrown into that small area in such a short period of time, that it was virtually impossible to sum up what happened there for the average visitor to Gettysburg.

Indeed.

But since that time several books have been written that help to sort out the confused fighting in Mr. Rose's wheatfield that was part of the much larger tactical movement conceived by Confederate commander General Robert E. Lee to attack the Union line along Cemetery Ridge and cost both sides so many casualties.

The book *Gettysburg's Bloody Wheatfield* by Jay Jorgensen and its derivative work, *The Wheatfield at Gettysburg: A Walking Tour* concentrate on the three-plus hours of combat in and close to the Wheatfield. Yet, even Jorgensen was forced to admit the nature of the fighting was "confusing, overlapping" with nineteen total brigades maneuvering through the wheat and up and down the undulating ground.

Beginning at 4:00 P.M., after the half-hour Confederate artillery bombardment, Major General John B. Hood's troops struck Sickles' men at Devil's Den and Little Round Top, on and beyond Sickles' left flank. In about 40 minutes of fighting, Confederates drove Union troops from a stone wall on the south edge of Mr. Rose's wheatfield. Hand-to-hand combat indicated the ferocity of the fighting and the battle spread into Rose's woods.

Less than an hour later Confederates continued their attack into the southern part of the Wheatfield and toward a small rise named Stony Hill. Union brigades were ordered into the area to blunt the southern attack but were pushed back.

Additional northern troops drove the Confederates back. One Union commander, Colonel Edward Cross, speaking with his aide the night before, confessed a premonition of his own death. The aide tried to assuage his fears, but remembered Cross just before entering the battle tying a black scarf on his head rather than his customary red one and thought it strange. Major General Winfield S. Hancock saw Cross as he advanced into the battle and told him this would be his last fight without a star—meaning a promotion from colonel to brigadier general. "No General," Cross said solemnly, "this is my last battle." A short time later he was indeed mortally wounded where the monument to the 5th New Hampshire now stands. According to Harry Pfanz in his book, *Gettysburg: The Second Day*, Lieutenant Colonel Charles E. Hapgood, commanding the 5th, saw the shot fired from behind the boulder about 40 yards to their front and ordered Sergeant Charles Phelps to shoot the man who wounded Cross. Phelps waited patiently until the man reloaded and popped up from behind the rock, then shot him. That rock can be seen today across from the 5th New Hampshire Monument.

Fifth New Hampshire Regimental Monument

Hancock's promise of a promotion went unfulfilled. Cross died wishing he could have seen the country peaceful again and believing that "the boys"—the men he commanded—would miss him.

Union Brigadier General Samuel Zook was on horseback leading his men in an attack upon Stony Hill. Thus a conspicuous target, he took a bullet to the stomach just after he crossed the Wheatfield Road and, still mounted but reeling unsteadily in the saddle, was led off the field by his aides. He died the next day.

It was about this time that the famed Irish Brigade, having just been given general absolution and reminded by Father William Corby that the Catholic Church would refuse Christian burial to any soldier who turns his back to the enemy or deserts his flag, marched into the whirlpool of the Wheatfield.

The Confederate officer corps was also taking losses.

South Carolina colonel William DeSaussure, leading his unit in on foot was struck in the thigh, a wound that would eventually kill him.

Confederate Brigadier General Paul Jones Semmes was also mortally wounded in the fighting. Semmes was quite accomplished, according to Jay Jorgensen in his book *Gettysburg's Bloody Wheatfield*. In his late forties, Semmes was a prominent banker and plantation owner in Georgia. Just prior to the outbreak of the war, he was sent to New York City by the governor of Georgia to purchase, of all things, military supplies for the expected conflict. He bought some $93,000 worth from the willing entrepreneurial New Yorkers. Going into battle he wore a red turban on his head, no doubt making him conspicuous in a sea of butternut and gray uniforms and caps.

He too, apparently had felt the cold breath of fate on his way northward toward Pennsylvania. While denying any "presentment" of death, he realized that he had already exceeded "the average number of battles unharmed, I ought not to count on much further immunity." A week before the battle he wrote a letter to a friend asking that his life insurance policy be renewed.

Sadly, it proved to be $863.00 well spent. He was mortally wounded fighting in the Wheatfield.

Visitors to Gettysburg, and particularly those interested in taking our ghost tours, often ask if they will see a ghost. Obviously, the ghosts will usually not appear specifically on our request. As well, a cursory survey of all the stories in my books, shows that only about ten percent of ghostly experiences catalogued are "visuals." But just because you haven't *seen* a ghost at Gettysburg, doesn't mean you haven't *experienced* one.

Not surprisingly, all the human senses are involved in a potential ghostly experience.

About sixty percent of all the ghostly experiences recorded in my books are auditory. In other words, at Gettysburg you are more likely to hear a ghost than see one. Footsteps with no visible source are the most common auditory experience.

Perhaps the second most triggered human sense is olfactory—your sense of smell. People will report smelling old fashioned perfumes—lilac and rose water—perhaps a remnant phantom odor from when the women of Gettysburg loaded up their handkerchiefs for a walk outside, because one never knew when a change in the wind would blow the hideous stench of human bodies decomposing to assault one's nose. Rotten eggs are another out-of-place odor smelled by patrons of our tours. This foul smell may be the phantom remnant of the smell of burned black powder, the main propellant for firearms during the war, a major component of which was sulfur.

But from my "Lost Files" comes the story of another smell, even more frightening and hideous than old-fashioned perfume or rotten eggs rising from wherever to remind yet another visitor of the seemingly omnipresence at Gettysburg of death.

The corresponding individual revealed that he was a lover of Civil War history and curious about the possibility of otherworldly hauntings, but assured me that he was the most skeptical person one could meet. He happened to be visiting the Wheatfield during the month of July, walking the paths and taking as many photos as he could. Along one of the paths he was struck by the extremely strong odor of what could only be identified as blood. Shocked, he looked around for any evidence of a freshly-killed animal, but could find none. He said that it, in no way, smelled like decomposition, but instead reminded him of fresh blood, as if you had opened up a package of steaks from the grocery…only much stronger.

He said his friends told him it was probably just his imagination and so asked me if I have any information on what he smelled. Since his letter was in my "Lost Files," this is my response, albeit late. No doubt the odor he experienced was a paranormal remnant of the actual smell of the Wheatfield after the black powder smoke dissipated and all that was left were the hundreds of bodies of men and horses, still bleeding or having bled out, their life's blood pooling and thickening on the sunbaked ground or on exposed rocks in the hot July evening. With no worldly explanation, it could be no more, no less….

I received a letter about a year later from a woman who had ventured out to the Wheatfield around 7:00 P.M. one November evening. She said she wanted to visit because, for her, the spot had a "sad and strong sensation." She also admitted that she had had strange experiences before akin to psychic abilities that she recognized and accepted. While standing in the darkness in that fabled field of death, she saw dark forms moving through it, but from the flashes of their cameras realized that they were living beings. As a welcome interruption from the sadness she felt, she received a phone call.

I mention this because it is a psychological truism that, no matter what we try and tell ourselves, our brains just cannot "multi-task." One, if not both, of the tasks suffers for the effort. While attempting to answer questions and converse on the phone, our brain waves change, trying to remember or picture events from the past that we are discussing or plans for the near future we are making.

But it may just be these changes in brain waves caused by distracted focus that allow us to experience things we would not define as normal. Still conversing, she thought she saw two people nearby walking away from her. At first, she thought it might have been the two elderly ladies she'd seen a few minutes before, but realized that the two figures were walking far more slowly than the two ladies she had seen. One was bent over and she had the urge to interrupt her phone call to offer assistance to them. Looking back at the road she saw that the car she had seen the two ladies arrive in, had left. She studied the figures more carefully and, through the darkness and slight background light, she realized the one wore a kepi and had a soldier's field pack strapped to his back. She now thought that she had identified them as reenactors...until they, in her words, "seemed to notice me and disappeared in front of me." She insisted that, in spite of this otherworldly activity in a field that was once, for a few loathsome hours in the past, an otherworldly hell on earth, she, somehow, had not been scared.

Can animals detect ghosts? If you are a domestic animal owner, no doubt you have noticed—often to your amusement—all the silly, unexplainable things pets do. It is part of their charm.

But there are other times when they act strangely, as if they see something that we cannot. Depending upon where that activity occurs, they could be seeing remnant spirit energy—a ghost.

Somewhere in my files I have a photo of the dog of a friend taken during a paranormal convention. Before the photo was snapped the dog was acting kind of weird, as if there were some tiny unseen insects landing on his back, twisting his neck to chase them away. My friend took a picture of him. In the screen could be seen five or six "orbs" floating around his back.

Now everyone has a theory about orbs. I won't get into all the explanations of just what they are—dust too close to the camera lens, moisture in the air, perhaps even actual paranormal energy—but the dog seemed to be reacting to something touching him just as the camera caught the "orbs" moving around him. One of the reasons given for animals' sensitivity to ghosts is that they have fur, which is sensitive to electromagnetic energy or static in the air. It is also why electromagnetic field (EMF) meters and other devices sensitive to EMFs (REM pods, etc.) seemingly detect ghosts.

Perhaps this electromagnetic component is also why ghosts can create "EVP"—Electronic Voice Phenomena—voices captured on recorders which, since they are not heard when they are recorded, are believed to be electromagnetic in nature.

But then there are other times when your animal may stare into an empty corner or section of wall ignoring your commands to get their attention. Sometimes their stare even follows something invisible as it appears to move. One possible explanation is that an animal's eyes are more sensitive to broader spectrums of visible light, which is why they can see better in the dark or react to motion more quickly than humans. Many paranormal theorists believe that these expanded spectrums of light—into the infra-red or ultra-violet—are the frequencies in which spirit energies can be seen.

Animals' ability to react to ghosts also seems to depend upon where they are. A haunted location seems to help. A haunted location like the Wheatfield at Gettysburg....

A woman who owns three show dogs brought them to the Wheatfield one evening just as it was getting dark. As she exited the car to look around, she took only one of the dogs with her. The other two were used to being left in the car, just like they had been many times earlier in the evening. However, within a few seconds of her and her one dog leaving, the other two dogs started whimpering loudly. She turned and told the usually obedient dogs to quiet down so as not to disturb other visitors to the Wheatfield, but within a few seconds the two dogs in the car began to howl.

Her dogs never howled before and being show dogs and used to being in the car, never fussed when left alone. Just a few minutes before they arrived at the Wheatfield, at another site, she had left them in the car and they had been silent.

Though she had obviously heard other dogs howl, she called their howling "weird" and "just too eerie." She finally turned to head back to the car to quiet them, taking pictures just in case something was near them, but nothing showed up in the photos. The dogs were quiet for the rest of the time she was there. Perhaps, she wondered, something else had been approaching the car that they sensed? If there was, it was something that she could not see nor photograph.

Writers attempt to be objective when producing their craft. Sometimes in the "ghost business" that is impossible, especially when a paranormal event happens to the writer. This story from fellow author and dear friend Patty Wilson reminds us of one more way ghosts can make their presence known: by forceful physical attack.

Writing in her book, *The Pennsylvania Ghost Guide,* Vol. 1, she recounted a story of something that happened to her and her then-husband during a visit to the Wheatfield.

They had spent a good part of their day touring the battlefield. Her brother was the accompanying photographer and was snapping numerous photos on his professional-grade 35 mm camera. She was aware of the battlefield's unexplainable reputation for draining batteries and therefore packed extras. She had also heard that cameras sometimes just stopped functioning for no reason at all.

Their time was getting close to an appointment Patty had scheduled to do an interview, so they decided to make one more stop at the Wheatfield. Her brother got out of the car to snap some shots, but his high-end camera would not work. He fiddled with it and realized that whenever he took a shot of something like the distant mountains or a building on the battlefield outside the Wheatfield, the camera operated normally. Aimed into that field of death...nothing.

He returned to the car and explained the problem. Patty's husband, realizing they were pressed for time, grabbed her camera from the seat and walked out into the Wheatfield. They had used the camera through four rolls of film and reloaded just twenty minutes before. Only four shots had been taken.

Within a few seconds he was back at the car. He tried to take a picture but the camera instantly rewound itself to the beginning of the roll. They had owned and used the camera for over a year. Nothing like this had ever happened. Her brother commented that "There's something about that field."

Clearly frustrated, Patty's husband grabbed the small 110 camera they always carried for backup. "I'll get you a picture of that field," he said defiantly, and marched out to his vantage point, where the backup camera clicked off several pictures. He got back in the van and they drove to the interview.

Along the route, Patty's husband began complaining about his arm hurting, finally taking off his heavy outer shirt to discover a long red welt on the underside of his upper arm. Try as they might, they couldn't remember anything he had done on the trip that could have caused it.

Patty did her interview, then came to our *Ghosts of Gettysburg Tour Headquarters* to sign her books for customers for a couple of hours. Meantime, her husband and brother took a walk through town. As they passed one of the ghost tour guides on the street, they overheard them saying to their customers that one of the ways a ghost may be detected is through old fashioned smells that have no obvious source, such as tobacco smoke. Skeptics that they are—or perhaps were—they chuckled at the hype some tour guides use to entertain their customers and continued to explore the streets. They were standing off the main thoroughfare of Steinwehr Avenue, admiring the parked antique buses used by one company for taking tourists around the battlefield.

Suddenly, they were engulfed by the heavy smell of pipe tobacco. Looking around, they saw no one near—no one in the lot, no one behind the buses. They even made a point of trying to find the smoker, going so far as to walk back out onto the street, to no avail. But once out onto the street, in spite of the fact that there were no smokers near, the smell grew strong again.

A few steps down the street and the smell vanished…only to waft up in their faces a few minutes later. Again, they could not discern a source.

If Patty's husband returned home to mid-western Pennsylvania with a little less skepticism about the supernatural than before his trip to Gettysburg, what happened at home may have convinced him even more of the presence of entities from another not-so-distant dimension.

He had just finished showering and was getting dressed when he said to Patty, "Did you ever hear of a ghost hurting anyone?"

"No," she said. "Mark Nesbitt may have. Why?"

He pulled back the sleeve of his T-shirt and showed her a series of bruises on the underside of his upper arm in the shape of a hand-print—fingers and a thumb. They were in the same area as the red welt was the day before. Now, a hand-shaped bruise replaced the welt.

Patty's mind went through all the possibilities: the print was in a spot where he couldn't have done it himself; it was obviously very forceful pressure that produced it which he would have felt and mentioned, but didn't; the long red welt was gone, replaced inexplicably by the compact bruise—impossible in one day.

"I think we'd better call Mark," he said.

As Patty wrote: "Suddenly my ex-military, very skeptical husband wasn't sounding so skeptical anymore."

I remember Patty's call. I told her that I'd heard of people being tapped, touched or pushed, even caressed in a loving way, but never bruised, and suggested she get a photo.

She took several quick photos. Several days later she was talking to her brother who indicated incredulity and told her that he had noticed something, but blew it off until she told him about her husband's bruise. He was getting dressed sometime after returning from Gettysburg. He said he noticed on his left calf about four inches below his knee, "a big bruise like someone had grabbed me there." He reminded her that he doesn't bruise easily. "I can't imagine how it got there. It's just a big hand print like someone grabbed me real hard and dug in."

Patty writes of the family's strange experience—just one of many to come for her—as one who experienced the events first hand, so I quote from her story "A Trip to Gettysburg," from her book, *The Pennsylvania Ghost Guide,* Vol. 1:

"I only know that two sane, skeptical men both smelled phantom pipe smoke three separate times and both men who had walked upon the Wheat Field came away with a bruise as a souvenir of their journey into a battle which many say is still being fought by the dead. Did a phantom grab at them to prevent them from taking a photograph? I don't have answers, only questions, and I suppose that I am in good company."

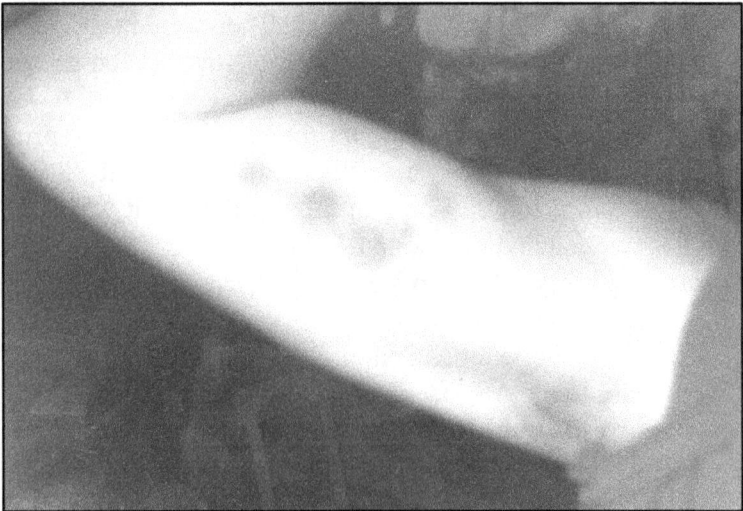

Bruised Arm
Photo Courtesy of Patty Wilson

THE NOISY GHOSTS OF GETTYSBURG

There are horrors beyond horrors, and this was one of those nuclei of all dreamable hideousness which the cosmos saves to blast an accursed and unhappy few.

—H. P. Lovecraft

Imagine this: You are walking alone down darkened Carlisle Street in Gettysburg. It is late at night. There is no traffic. You are well aware of the sordid, violent history of the street. Thousands of Union troops retreated down it, chased by victorious Confederates on July 1, 1863; men were shot down, wounded and killed along the very roadway where you walk. But tonight, over a century-and-a-half after the slaughter, it is quiet. The autumn wind has been chilly but the rattling of dead leaves blowing down the street has died down. It is so quiet now you can hear the footsteps of the person coming up behind you. You slow up to let them pass, but when you do, no one passes. Why not? Because no one is there….

Confused, you quicken your pace. The place you're staying for the night is within sight. You had heard it was once used as a hospital during the battle, housing the suffering wounded soldiers and those who will suffer no more, and that it might be haunted…no, this is not the time to think about that.

You hurry through the door and it gives a reassuring, solid kerthunk as it closes securely behind you. You twist the deadbolt, hook the security chain and begin to smile at yourself for having such a vivid imagination.

You crawl into bed and turn out the light, ready for a good night's sleep. You're just dozing off when the light flashes back on. What the…?

You get out of the warm bed and go over to the light switch. You swore you turned it off—in fact, it is in the off position—but somehow the light came back on. You flick the switch a couple of times and the light goes off and on, finally enveloping you again in total darkness. You nervously mumble something about "old fashioned wiring," and try to fall asleep again.

Just as you are dozing off again, somewhere in that netherworld between sleep and wakefulness, in that place that must be as close to death as we can get and still be alive, you hear it, loud enough to assure you that you are definitely not dreaming. From downstairs it comes:

Kerthunk!

A poltergeist, according to Rosemary Ellen Guiley, is "a mischievous and sometimes malevolent spirit or unknown energy that is characterized by noises, moving objects, and physical disturbances." The word *poltergeist* is German for "to knock" (*poltern*) and "ghost" (*geist*). Historical accounts of poltergeist activity have been found from ancient Roman times up to the present day. Not surprisingly, Gettysburg, as well, has its share of "noisy ghosts."

I have recorded scores of examples of poltergeist activity at Gettysburg—actually have been the percipient of some poltergeist activity myself—and never, until now, realized what an important thing it is in proving the existence of ghosts and of life after death.

There seems to always have been, throughout our history, at least the feeling that we humans are more than just a body and brain, that we have some intangible thing inside of us which we sometimes call "spirit" or "soul." Certainly, the Victorians of the Civil War Era who espoused Christianity were convinced that there was a second part to this life besides just the physical bodies we walk around in. Civil War soldiers' heartbroken wives, mothers, sisters and daughters fed the fires of what came to be known as Spiritualism by striving, often through "mediums," to contact husbands, sons, brothers and fathers slain in the killing fields from Pennsylvania to Texas to Florida and warring states in between.

In fact, it was my own experiences with poltergeist activity at Gettysburg that inadvertently led to the writing of the first *Ghosts of Gettysburg* book, hence to the multi-volume series and numerous other books and television programs.

It happened in the Culp Farmhouse, when I was on patrol one fall night. I was called there by the resident— the superintendent of the park himself. By the stomping of heavy boots down the hall on the second floor, he and his family were convinced they had a prowler. I got there just as the stomping had ended. We went out to the side where it was a potentially leg-breaking drop from the window where the "prowler" had to have exited to the ground and there was no one either lying injured from the fall or hobbling off across the open field.

There was the door to the attic in the historic Weikert House that I'd heard would never stay shut. The tenant who lived there before me even nailed it shut with a small brad one night; the next morning it was open. I too, when I lived in the picturesque fieldstone farmhouse just south of the majestic Pennsylvania Monument around which so much human energy swirled on July 2, 1863, could not keep the door closed no matter how often I tried.

Even more dramatic were the unmistakable and unnerving sounds I heard when I lived in the Cemetery Lodge, the brick building just inside the iron gate of the National Cemetery:

One afternoon I was watching TV in the first floor living room while my housemate was reading upstairs in his room. My back was to the stairs, but I heard the familiar sound of someone coming down the stairs and pausing on the landing. The TV was quiet at the time and I wondered why my housemate stopped on the landing. I turned around and no one was there. I was so convinced that I had heard him that I walked upstairs, knocked on his door and opened it to see a bleary-eyed reader lounging on his bed. No, he said to my question, he hadn't come partially downstairs. He'd been right there reading and dozing.

Then there was the afternoon when I was cleaning up after my lunch, alone in the Lodge, taking plates to the kitchen. I heard the wail of a baby. It stopped me in my tracks. Explanations flew through my head: pipes moaning in the house? The building "settling"? No, it was a baby crying. That spectral noise was later confirmed by a former resident who had heard it several times herself.

Years later, there was the day I heard the drummer at the Triangular Field: four distinct taps on a drum. I waited for more. Having been a drummer, I identified the sound without a doubt and knew that there would be more taps—no drummer can resist. No living drummer, that is, for there were no more drum taps the next three or four minutes. Perhaps it was just some drummer boy, now long gone, attempting to get the attention of a kindred spirit.

From another house I lived in, but from a tenant:

In the Hummelbaugh House, just off the Taneytown Road, where Confederate general William Barksdale of Mississippi breathed his last and was temporarily buried, a poltergeist not once, but time and again, scattered valuable collectable salt dips from a shelf to the floor.

From the college come stories of the Sheads House on Carlisle Street rented to female students and a veritable den of one—or more—poltergeists:

After a day of moving in, the women had settled in the living room to relax. It was after dark when they heard the sounds of glass crashing to the floor in the dining room. They found a broom and were about to enter the darkened room to sweep up the glass when they heard footsteps crunching across it. Frightened, they summoned help from neighboring students with what they were sure was a prowler, then flicked on the light and discovered that not only was there no one walking in the room, but no broken glass on the floor.

Other poltergeist activity haunted the rest of their year in the house: loud, indescribable noises coming from inside walls; a voice shouting "stop," "don't do it"; two doors slamming shut despite a thick carpet underneath them; a woman hearing someone walking upstairs while she was alone; a woman tapped on her shoulder blade by an unseen hand; more footsteps and banging; the sounds of someone walking in a darkened bedroom; a muffled voice coming from an air vent.

It wasn't until later the possible source of the activity was discovered. The house sat at the confluence of three roads which focused the energy of panicked retreating Union troops followed closely by victorious rebels, the energy of the living and dying converging on the site of the house. As well, at least one wounded Union soldier, after being cared for by Mrs. Sheads, died in the house.

Just out Carlisle Street from the Sheads House is a fraternity house renovated into college offices:

Brothers in the Theta Chi House were randomly treated to lights flashing off, needing to be turned back on manually; footsteps echoing from empty rooms; rappings were heard and doors swung shut—or open— on their own on windless days; voices emanated from empty rooms; a full beer mug levitated from its place to mid-room where it dropped; so did a brandy snifter. All evidence of poltergeist activity.

On the college campus the story of a poltergeist comes from a security guard:

Late at night, patrolling his campus rounds, he was checking Glatfelter Hall, a classroom building. Suddenly he heard the random and bizarre sounds of chains rattling in the hallway. An investigation revealed no chains, but mysterious wet footprints across the hall, not from door to door, but from solid wall to solid wall.

Another women's housing facility named East Cottage seemed filled with noisy, mischievous spirits:

One night a woman watched incredulously as six books lifted over a lipped shelf one by one and fell to the floor; a precious Hummel-type music box lifted like the books off the same lipped shelf and was smashed to the floor; all the residents one night heard the old piano in the living room playing by itself; the key in the locked cellar door was seen to turn by itself and the door opened. No one emerged from the dark basement.

The James Gettys Hotel on Chambersburg Street seemed to have long-gone visitors out-of-time and space from its previous incarnation as a youth Hostel:

During rehab construction of the old, pre-battle period building, a worker's tool had been seen moving along the floor across a room by itself and a door closed, locking itself; workers were stunned when a rocker would periodically start rocking with no living being near it.

Then there is the famous Gettysburg and Northern Railroad engine house, scene of numerous personal paranormal investigations, sitting on land once fought over on July 1, 1863, where some of the estimated 800-1200 soldiers listed as "missing" from the rosters may still lie buried.

I was attempting an EVP session during a paranormal investigation in the engine house, when Patty Wilson, author and medium, felt that a man (dead) in the back of the building wanted to talk with me. I was already getting good results from the spirit I was communicating with and told her I would get to that person momentarily. Apparently, that wasn't good enough. Like a typical poltergeist, he kicked an orange traffic barrel from its place on a tire, where it had been sitting for weeks, partially onto the floor with a loud, very audible "thump."

One of the first stories I collected from the railroaders was of footsteps from an unseen source descending the interior wooden stairs. Later, during a paranormal investigation we were conducting, I heard heavy footsteps on the far side of one of the massive engines they had been working on. I investigated and there was no one walking on it. I asked the manager of the railroad if there were any liquids cooling in the engine to make noises. "No," was his reply. "Everything has been drained for repairs." We had heard from some of the workers that while repairing the old dining car, which sat on a track outside the engine house, a number of loud "bangs" were heard on the roof. Thorough investigations gave no clue as to what made the noise. During one investigation, the sound happened to my investigative team, with no evidence as to where the loud noise originated. Workers inside the engine house also witnessed a Styrofoam cup levitate out of a trashcan, float for a few seconds, then fall back into the can.

Also from the engine house comes the story, from a former manager, of a physical manifestation of a responsive spirit:

He was the last to leave the building one evening. He glanced at his desk and saw he had left his ceramic coffee cup in the middle instead of placing it to the side like he always did. Too tired to go back to his desk, he vowed to take care of it in the morning. The first to arrive the next morning, he went to move the cup and it was already moved to the side. That night, he purposefully placed the cup in the center of his desk. The next morning it was again moved to the side. That night he ran an experiment, placed the cup in the middle of the desk, wrote a note that said "Move it to the other side," and put the note face down on his desk. The next morning, he was, as usual, the first in, and the cup had been moved once again…to the other side of the desk.

And yet more stories come from the National Park:

Even the famous Eisenhower Farm is not immune to "noisy ghosts." Many of the rangers who worked there have heard the heavy mirrored closet doors in Mrs. Eisenhower's bedroom slam shut, when they were the only ones there. Aha, you say. Not a poltergeist, but the wind blowing the doors shut. Except that they are sliding doors.

In 1998, the *Ghosts of Gettysburg Candlelight Walking Tours* purchased the Civil War Era building on the corner of Baltimore and Breckenridge Street, just two and a half blocks south of the center Square of town. Little did we know (but we should have!) how haunted the house was, filled especially with poltergeists. Many of the events were chronicled in another chapter in this book.

Right off, we were told by a famous local psychic that we would be hearing children in the house. True to her prediction, residents of the second floor have heard balls being dribbled downstairs when we were closed for business and no one was in that section of the house.

There was the paranormal research group staying overnight that heard children playing in the back of the first floor and so set up their equipment there. No sooner had they set up when they heard the children playing in the front of the house. They tore down the equipment and set up in the front. Finally, the team leader placed a camera in the middle room of the house and, after scores of snapping pictures, finally got one of the best photos of a ghost I have ever seen. It was a child, of course! When I first bought the house, doors would open on their own, including some pantry doors I made sure were closed every time I saw them. Even when I knew no one had been in the house since my last visit, they were open.

In the past we have offered "learning weekends" to people interested in paranormal investigating. Of course we use our building as one of the investigation sites. This means that a number of people have witnessed the effects of our poltergeist activity.

One evening I was taking a group on a "walk-through" of the building to point out trip hazards, give a brief history of the building, and point out our paranormal "hotspots" where they should focus their activities before letting them investigate on their own. The group had just descended the inside stairs from the second floor. I was in the main room with most of the group. One man was at the bottom of the stairs. Suddenly he looked up the stairs and I heard three distinct footsteps at the top of the stairs.
"Is that your wife coming down?" I asked. "I don't want to start talking without her."
He shook his head and looked at me wide-eyed.
"She's down there with you."

"Then who's coming down the stairs?" I asked.

"Nobody," he answered.

I asked him if he heard the three footsteps and he said yes, that was why he had stopped: to see who was coming down. Several others in the group nearest the door also heard them. But no one—no one visible, at least—came down the stairs that night.

Sometimes we have friends stay overnight on the second floor of what has affectionately become known as "The Ghost House." They often mention hearing people coming up and down the stairs, even though they are the only ones— the only ones *alive,* that is—occupying the house.

It was in the back room where I began to notice something strange whenever I was attempting to gather EVP there. During our "Mysterious Journeys Weekends" where we taught paranormal investigating, I usually stood with my back to the door from the kitchen as I asked questions into my recorder. Of course we turned off the lights, more for effect and to allow everyone to concentrate their attention, not because ghosts only appear after dark. Trust me: nowhere is there a "ghost law" that orders they shall only be active after dark.

Per protocol, I would turn on the digital recorder, set on voice activation and ask my questions— "Are you a Confederate soldier from Georgia? Have you ever been to Atlanta?"—with a 30 to 40 second pause between questions while I stood in silence. The strange thing was, more often than not during a session, I would hear footsteps approaching me from the kitchen, behind my back. I sometimes would turn, thinking it was my wife Carol coming to tell me something, but I wouldn't see her, nor would I see anyone approaching. I sometimes mentioned it to the people in that room and several of them said they had heard the poltergeist's footsteps too. In fact, one participant sitting near me said that he thought he'd actually seen a face lean over my shoulder as if to see what was going on.

Then there was our guide who was stuck with her tour on the large side porch due to a heavy rainstorm who heard heavy footfalls both downstairs then overhead on the balcony mentioned earlier in this volume.

There's more documentation of poltergeist activity from "The Ghost House":

A sales rack of a dozen pendulums was set on the floor as an experiment by my wife Carol and another investigator. They started asking questions of the spirits in the house, particularly the child ghosts, and requested that they move the pendulums to indicate they were present. Suddenly, the pendulums began moving in response to questions from investigators. To check if the movement was truly paranormal and not caused by the floor moving, they placed a K-2 electromagnetic field meter under the pendulums as an experiment, to see if whatever was moving the pendulums gave off any electromagnetic energy. During the session, the K-2 began lighting up in response to the questions and the movement of the pendulums.

There are even some poltergeist cases from my recently discovered and unpublished "Lost Files."

A woman whose family frequently visits Gettysburg, wrote to me about two similar incidents that occurred—one in the Valley of Death and the other in the Triangular Field—of dangerous poltergeist activity. While standing on Crawford Avenue in the now peaceful valley below Little Round Top, a friend of hers was struck by a rock flying through the air when there was no one around them. A second incident was caught on video of a rock flying at them from over the fence. Again, no living being was visible as the thrower. After the thousands of stories from people visiting the battlefield and experiencing strange events, these are the only two I can recall with the potential for real harm.

But the most important questions remain: Why is poltergeist activity so important to the study of ghosts? How does the study of poltergeist activity on the battlefield at Gettysburg further the study of life after death?

Other than getting the living be-jeebers scared out of you when you're walking along one of the quiet battlefield roads and suddenly hear the boom of a long-gone cannon or a volley of phantom musketry from an invisible source—or have a rock thrown at you—there is much to be learned from these unique and obviously numerous types of paranormal phenomena.

In fact, poltergeist activity may be the very key to proving ghosts are indeed the remaining energy of the dead in as much as it is related to another paranormal phenomenon: Psychokinesis.

Psychokinesis, again defined by Rosemary Ellen Guiley, is "the mind's ability to affect the external world, often referred to as 'mind over matter.' Psychokinesis can occur either spontaneously or through an apparent projection of will."

In short, it is the willful moving of a physical object without physical contact, using the energy of the mind alone.

The source of psychokinesis is also problematic. Some say that it is generated by the mind of a living person. While some humans have shown the ability to move small, light objects under laboratory conditions, the living human brain apparently does not generate enough power to slam doors, rock chairs, or move tools across a floor. Or throw rocks.

But evidently, a spirit can generate that kind of energy.

My two very personal experiences with poltergeists, in addition to those mentioned above, came unexpectedly during dark nights: one in the cellar of the Cashtown Inn during an EVP session, when I was tapped three times on the back. Turning around, I saw no one behind me. A few seconds later, it came again—three distinct taps. Moments later, again: tap, tap, tap. I finally ended the session and asked the group of investigators if they had seen anyone behind me. The universal answer was, no.

Over the years, paranormal researchers have performed experiments on living individuals who possess psychokinetic abilities to determine whether it may be electromagnetic energy moving objects in psychokinesis trials. At least one laboratory confirmed the increase of *magnetic* fields in the vicinity of the living individuals, as well as recording enhanced psychokinetic abilities during magnetic disturbances caused by sunspots. The scientists theorized that one of the external "energy body fields," possibly related to the aura fields humans possess, vibrates: "If the *frequency of vibration* of this field is stepped up, energy or information from another 'dimension' can come through us."

Energy or information from another dimension? As in the place where spirits dwell?

And the other distinct personal instance of poltergeist activity happened to me at the Daniel Lady Farm during a night-time séance circle. As I stood observing the participants attempting to contact dead soldiers, I felt the sleeve of my shirt pulled forcefully downward. Thinking it may have been my wife trying silently to get my attention, I turned quickly to see no one near me. Nor was I moving near anything to snag it. As if to prove what it was—a poltergeist—in the barnyard once filled with dead and wounded Confederate soldiers, it tugged my sleeve again.

But here's the real importance of psychokinesis and so much poltergeist activity at Gettysburg:

If poltergeist activity—physical manifestations in this world—can be attributed to surviving human consciousness, it could be considered evidence of the reality of life after death and proof of what we call ghosts.

According to author Stacy Horn in her book *Unbelievable,* J. B. Rhine who, for 50 years led the Duke University

Parapsychological Laboratory, believed that psychokinesis "was the next logical step in proving the mind's independence from the body and therefore life after death."

Addressing the subject from the skeptic's point of view, Rhine continued: "If the mind was powerless to affect the material world after the brain died, life after death was not possible."

Rhine went on: "If the mind is different from the physical brain system it *could* have a different destiny." Meaning the destiny of a "life" after death: what we define as a ghost.

Yet modern science has, for a long time, been dumbfounded by consciousness that would encompass the functions of "mind." Part of the problem is that science is not even certain as to *where* consciousness is located.

Mainstream "materialistic" science had formerly located consciousness in the physical brain, although when tests are done, they cannot exactly pinpoint where it originates or where it is stored. Modern neurosurgery has shown that consciousness does not reside in some specific section of the biological brain. Modern psychology and physics may back that up.

Many Eastern philosophers and religions believe in a universal consciousness with the astounding and unique attribute that everything humans have ever done, thought or felt *throughout time* has been recorded on what they call the Akashic Records, also called the Akashic Field.

This concept of a "field," which is invisible and yet all around us, containing all the records of human existence reminds us of the theory that some of our brain tasks, such as memory, learning, and, of course, paranormal functions of the brain, indicate that the brain is not so much like a recorder than it is like a radio receiver "tuning into" the Akashic Field for data and information.

All humans need to do is learn how to tune their brains to the frequency of the Akashic Field and the wisdom of the ages is theirs.

So, if consciousness is not dependent upon the flesh and blood brain to exist, it confirms the "survival theory"—that the personality or consciousness survives the physical death of the body and some of the contents and experiences of our lives contained in our brain are already stored in another space or dimension other than the one we occupy in life. In other words, "backed-up" like our computers in the "cloud" of the Akashic Field.

Which is where visitors to Gettysburg come in.

They come by the hundreds of thousands—perhaps as many as a million—over the course of one year. Many of them witness poltergeist activity on the battlegrounds. Why is it important?

Because the existence of poltergeist activity as is readily and commonly experienced in and around Gettysburg, seems to prove that ghosts, as human consciousness with the ability to affect things in this world from another world, also exist.

Because no battle is ever won…. The field only reveals to man his own folly and despair, and victory is an illusion of philosophers and fools.

—William Faulkner

ACKNOWLEDGMENTS

Barbara and Robert Barber, Jeffery E. Benson, Corrine Brownholtz, Val and Tony Capone, Kelli Carpenter, Christi Caughman, Gregory Coco, Rich Cox, L. J. Cunningham, Don Drybola, Blair W. Fisher, Caroline Haag, Glen Hayes, Donna and Jim Hoey, Jeff Kaminski, Marie E. Kniffen, Darlene Krawczyk, Christine Kucklinca, Chris Lausch, Dave MacGregor, David Milburn, Kayla and Eric Miner, Shay Mullins, Margie Murray, Chris Nett, Ismael Nieves, Jeff Prechtel, George and Nancy Rambow, Jeff Ritzman, Derek Rush, Susan Schmitt, Kathy Shields, Sue Walters, Jan Sapp Watters, Tracy Weimer.

ABOUT THE AUTHOR

I started my career in Gettysburg as a National Park Service Ranger/Historian back in the 1970s. I knew that I wanted to be a writer, so after five years with the NPS, I got the crazy idea that I should start my own research and writing company. I became fascinated by, and started collecting, the ghost stories of the Gettysburg area. My first *Ghosts of Gettysburg* book came out in 1991. Since then, I have written over twenty books covering topics of historical interest, as well as the paranormal. My stories have been seen on *The History Channel, A&E, The Discovery Channel, The Travel Channel, Unsolved Mysteries, The Biography Channel*, and numerous regional television shows and heard on *Coast to Coast AM*, and regional radio.

In 1994, I started the commercially successful *Ghosts of Gettysburg Candlelight Walking Tours.*

Other books in print and/or ebooks by Mark Nesbitt:
Ghosts of Gettysburg
Ghosts of Gettysburg II
Ghosts of Gettysburg III
Ghosts of Gettysburg IV

Mark Nesbitt

Ghosts of Gettysburg V
Ghosts of Gettysburg VI
Ghosts of Gettysburg VII
Ghosts of Gettysburg VIII

Gettysburg's Hidden Haunted Hotspots: Spirits,
  Apparitions and Haunted Places on and off the
  Battlefield
Civil War Ghost Trails
A Ghost Hunters Field Guide: Gettysburg & Beyond
Fredericksburg & Chancellorsville: A Ghost Hunters
  Field Guide
Haunted Pennsylvania
The Big Book of Pennsylvania Ghost Stories

Cursed in Pennsylvania
Cursed in Virginia

Blood & Ghosts: Haunted Crime Scene Investigations
Haunted Crime Scenes

If The South Won Gettysburg
35 Days to Gettysburg: The Campaign Diaries of Two
  American Enemies (Reprinted as The Gettysburg
  Diaries: War Journals of Two American
  Adversaries)
Rebel Rivers: A Guide to Civil War Sites on the
  Potomac, Rappahannock, York, and James
Saber and Scapegoat: J.E.B. Stuart and the Gettysburg
  Controversy
Through Blood and Fire: The Selected Civil War
  Papers of Major General Joshua Chamberlain

Connect with **Mark Nesbitt** on Social Media:
  facebook.com/mark.v.nesbitt
  markvnesbitt.wordpress.com

www.ingramcontent.com/pod-product-compliance
Lightning Source LLC
Chambersburg PA
CBHW060251050426
42448CB00009B/1613